Crystallization-Study
of the
Psalms

Volume Four

Witness Lee

# The Holy Word for Morning Revival

*Living Stream Ministry*
Anaheim, CA • www.lsm.org

© 2012 Living Stream Ministry

First Edition, February 2012.

ISBN 978-0-7363-6116-3

Published by

*Living Stream Ministry*
2431 W. La Palma Ave., Anaheim, CA 92801 U.S.A.
P. O. Box 2121, Anaheim, CA 92814 U.S.A.

*Printed in the United States of America*

12  13  14  15 / 5  4  3  2  1

# Contents

## *Preface*

1. This book is intended as an aid to believers in developing a daily time of morning revival with the Lord in His word. At the same time, it provides a limited review of the winter training held December 26-31, 2011, in Anaheim, California, on the "Crystallization-study of the Psalms." Through intimate contact with the Lord in His word, the believers can be constituted with life and truth and thereby equipped to prophesy in the meetings of the church unto the building up of the Body of Christ.

2. The entire content of this book is taken from the *Crystallization-study Outlines: The Psalms (2)*, the text and footnotes of the Recovery Version of the Bible, selections from the writings of Witness Lee and Watchman Nee, and *Hymns*, all of which are published by Living Stream Ministry.

3. The book is divided into weeks. One training message is covered per week. Each week presents first the message outline, followed by six daily portions, a hymn, and then some space for writing. The training outline has been divided into days, corresponding to the six daily portions. Each daily portion covers certain points and begins with a section entitled "Morning Nourishment." This section contains selected verses and a short reading that can provide rich spiritual nourishment through intimate fellowship with the Lord. The "Morning Nourishment" is followed by a section entitled "Today's Reading," a longer portion of ministry related to the day's main points. Each day's portion concludes with a short list of references for further reading and some space for the saints to make notes concerning their spiritual inspiration, enlightenment, and enjoyment to serve as a reminder of what they have received of the Lord that day.

4. The space provided at the end of each week is for composing a short prophecy. This prophecy can be composed by considering all of our daily notes, the "harvest" of our inspirations during the week, and preparing a main point with

some sub-points to be spoken in the church meetings for the organic building up of the Body of Christ.

5. Following the last week in this volume, we have provided reading schedules for both the Old and New Testaments in the Recovery Version with footnotes. These schedules are arranged so that one can read through both the Old and New Testaments of the Recovery Version with footnotes in two years.

6. As a practical aid to the saints' feeding on the Word throughout the day, we have provided verse cards at the end of the volume, which correspond to each day's scripture reading. These may be cut out and carried along as a source of spiritual enlightenment and nourishment in the saints' daily lives.

7. *Crystallization-study Outlines: The Psalms (2)* was compiled by Living Stream Ministry from the writings of Witness Lee and Watchman Nee. The outlines, footnotes, and cross-references in the Recovery Version of the Bible are by Witness Lee. All of the other references cited in this publication are from the published ministry of Witness Lee and Watchman Nee.

# CRYSTALLIZATION-STUDY
## OF THE PSALMS

Banners:

Whenever God's people exalt Christ,
giving Him the preeminence
in every aspect of their living,
there is restoration and revival.

To take God as our habitation,
our eternal dwelling place,
is the highest and fullest
experience of God.

God's heart is set on Zion,
the city of God, with Christ within it,
and on Zion we have the church
as the Body of Christ
and God's economy for His testimony.

The praise in the Psalms
issues in the consummate praise
with Hallelujahs
because the earth
has been fully recovered by God
and brought under the reign of Christ
with the kingdom.

### Christ as the Cornerstone for God's Building

Scripture Reading: Psa. 118:22-26; Isa. 28:16; Matt. 21:42; Acts 4:10-12; Eph. 2:20-22; 1 Pet. 2:4-7

*Day 1*  **I. Christ is not only the Lamb for redemption; He is also the stone for God's building (Psa. 118:22-26; Isa. 28:16; John 1:29; Acts 4:10-12).**

**II. In the Bible Christ is revealed as at least nine kinds of stones:**

A. He is the eternal rock (Isa. 26:4; Matt. 16:18), the foundation stone (Isa. 28:16; 1 Cor. 3:11), the living stone (1 Pet. 2:4), the cornerstone (Psa. 118:22; Isa. 28:16; 1 Pet. 2:6; Acts 4:11; Eph. 2:20), the precious stone (Isa. 28:16; 1 Pet. 2:4, 6-7), the topstone (Zech. 4:7), the cleft rock (Exo. 17:6; 1 Cor. 10:4), the crushing stone (Dan. 2:34-35; Matt. 21:44b), and the stone of stumbling (Isa. 8:14; Rom. 9:33).

B. We need to experience Christ as a stone in all positive aspects; if we experience Him in these aspects, we will have a complete building—a building that is actually Christ Himself (1 Pet. 2:4-5, 7).

*Day 2*  **III. In Psalm 118:22-26 Christ is revealed as the cornerstone:**

A. "The stone which the builders rejected / Has become the head of the corner," the chief cornerstone (v. 22; Matt. 21:42):

1. This stone is Christ, who is for God's building (Isa. 28:16; Zech. 3:9).

2. The builders are the Jewish leaders, who should have been working on God's building (Matt. 21:42).

3. When the Jewish builders rejected Christ, they rejected Him as the cornerstone, the One who would join the Gentiles to them into a holy temple in the Lord (Eph. 2:20-22).

4. In Ephesians 2:20 we see Christ as the cornerstone that joins together the two walls, one wall being the Jewish believers, and the other, the Gentile believers.

*Day 3*
*&*
*Day 4*

5. Christ as the cornerstone is for the building up of the church in the New Testament age (Matt. 16:18; Eph. 2:20-22; 1 Pet. 2:5):
   a. For the building up of the church as the temple of God, we need to experience Christ as the cornerstone (vv. 6-7).
   b. To God, Christ as the cornerstone is precious, and to us He is the preciousness (Matt. 21:42; Acts 4:11; 1 Pet. 2:4, 6-7).
   c. In Christ, the cornerstone, all the building, including both the Jewish and the Gentile believers, is growing into a holy temple in the Lord (Eph. 2:20-22).

B. "This is the day that Jehovah has made; / Let us exult and rejoice in it" (Psa. 118:24):
   1. This day is the day of Christ's resurrection; on the day of His resurrection the Lord Jesus was made the cornerstone by God (Acts 4:10-12).
   2. Christ was chosen by God in eternity past to be the cornerstone for God's spiritual building (1 Pet. 1:20; 2:4).
   3. However, the Jewish leaders as the builders rejected Christ to the uttermost, to such an extent that they put Him on the cross (Matt. 21:38-42a).
   4. God chose Christ as the cornerstone a second time in Christ's resurrection, thereby confirming His initial choosing of Christ in eternity past (Acts 4:10-12).
   5. After God resurrected Christ, God uplifted Him to the heavens in His ascension (Luke 24:51; Acts 1:9):
      a. Christ's ascension to Zion in the heavens was a further confirmation that God had chosen Him to be the cornerstone (Rev. 14:1; Isa. 28:16; 1 Pet. 2:6).
      b. Both Christ's resurrection and ascension prove and confirm that He is the head of the corner for God's building (Acts 2:24, 32, 36).

C. As the all-inclusive stone, Christ is the centrality of God's move for the building up of His eternal habitation (Matt. 21:42, 44; Zech. 3:9; 4:7; cf. Rev. 5:6; Acts 4:10-12; Isa. 28:16; Eph. 2:20-22; 1 Pet. 2:4-8; Dan. 2:34-35; Rev. 21:11; cf. 4:3):

1. Everything Christ is, everything He has done, and everything He is doing are due to the fact that He is the cornerstone (Eph. 2:20; 4:15-16).

2. It is by His being the cornerstone that He could die for us, that we could be crucified with Him, made alive with Him, resurrected with Him, and seated with Him in the heavenlies, and that He could save us, transform us into precious stones, and build us together to be God's habitation, God's unique temple in the universe (Gal. 2:20; Eph. 2:5-6, 20-22).

D. In God's New Testament economy Christ as the cornerstone, in His saving us (Acts 4:10-12), first makes us living stones for the building up of God's spiritual house (Matt. 16:18; John 1:42; 1 Pet. 2:4-7) and then, in the process of His transforming us (Rom. 12:2a; 2 Cor. 3:18), builds us up into a dwelling place of God (Eph. 2:19-22) so that He may carry out God's eternal economy for God's good pleasure (1:9; 3:9-11).

E. Prosperity in Psalm 118:25 typifies not material prosperity but the heavenly, spiritual, and divine blessings given to us by the Triune God, as described in Ephesians 1:3-14, which come to us by Christ's being the cornerstone.

*Day 5*  **IV. The whole book of Matthew is for the purpose that Christ would be the cornerstone for the building up of God's house (21:42; 1:21, 23; 2:2, 23; 3:17; 4:16; 12:6, 41-42; 16:16, 18, 27-28; 17:1-2, 5; 25:6):**

A. The Lord Jesus came not merely to be the Redeemer but to be the cornerstone for God's building (1:21; 21:42).

B. The Lord said that He would build His church, but

the religious ones rejected Him as the cornerstone
for God's building, and thus they could not be a part
of the building of God (16:18; 21:42).

C. As revealed in the Gospel of Matthew, the Father's
will is to build up the church with Christ as the rock
and the cornerstone (6:10; 7:21; 12:50):

1. The desire of God's heart is to have a dwelling
place on earth constituted with Christ and
according to Christ (Eph. 1:5, 9; 2:20-22).

*Day 6*

2. The Lord's word about "a city situated upon a
mountain" indicates that God's intention is
the building (Matt. 5:14):

a. This shining light is not an individual believer; the light is a corporate city built up
as one entity to shine over the people surrounding it (Rev. 21:23-24a).

b. In order to be a shining city, we must keep
the oneness and be built up as the church,
the Body of Christ, in Christ as the cornerstone (Matt. 16:18; 21:42; Eph. 4:1-6; 5:8-9).

V. **"Blessed is He who comes in the name of Jehovah; / We bless you from the house of Jehovah"**
**(Psa. 118:26):**

A. The first time that Christ came in the name of
Jehovah is mentioned in Matthew; however, He
was rejected by the Jewish builders (21:5-11, 42).

B. When the Lord Jesus comes the second time, the
Jews will again welcome Him warmly with these
words; this is the time when all the remnant of
Israel will turn and believe in Him and be saved
(23:39; Rom. 11:23, 26; Zech. 12:10).

### Morning Nourishment

**Isa.** **...Indeed I lay a stone in Zion as a foundation, a tested**
**28:16** **stone, a precious cornerstone *as a* foundation firmly**
**established; he who believes will not hasten away.**
**Acts** **This is the stone which was considered as nothing**
**4:11-12** **by you, the builders, which has become the head of**
**the corner. And there is salvation in no other, for**
**neither is there another name under heaven given**
**among men in which we must be saved.**

The Bible reveals that Christ is both the Lamb and the stone
(John 1:29; Acts 4:10-11). It is quite common for Christians to
praise the Lord and say, "Worthy is the Lamb! Hallelujah to the
Lamb! Glory to the Lamb! Praise the Lamb!" But have you ever
heard someone praise Him by saying, "Hallelujah to the stone!
Worthy is the stone! Praise the stone! Glory to the stone!" It seems
that historic Christianity does not know Christ as the stone or
praise Him as such....All Christians realize that the Lord Jesus
is the Savior, but very few realize that He is also the stone. He is
both the crucified Lamb and the rejected stone.

Christian theology repeatedly emphasizes the fundamental
matter of redemption. However, the theologians do not see
the matter of the building, and thus they do not talk about
it....Christ is not only the Lamb for redemption; He is also the
stone for the building. The building, not redemption, is the goal.
Redemption is part of the process to reach the goal. (*The Kernel
of the Bible,* pp. 108-109)

### Today's Reading

In the Bible Christ is revealed as at least nine kinds of stones.
He is the eternal rock (Isa. 26:4; Matt. 16:18), the foundation
stone (Isa. 28:16; 1 Cor. 3:11), the living stone (1 Pet. 2:4), the cornerstone (v. 6; Acts 4:11; Eph. 2:20; Psa. 118:22; Isa. 28:16), the
precious stone (v. 16; 1 Pet. 2:4, 6-7), the topstone (Zech. 4:7), the
cleft rock (Exo. 17:6; 1 Cor. 10:4), the crushing stone (Dan. 2:34-35;
Matt. 21:44b), and the stone of stumbling (Isa. 8:14; Rom. 9:33).

In ancient times the Jews built their dwellings with three main kinds of stones: a foundation stone, a cornerstone, and a top-stone....The Jewish method of construction was to make the foundation with a large rock, then to set up the cornerstone as a support, the equivalent of today's column, and to finish by placing the topstone as the roof. We should recognize that today the topstone has not yet been placed on God's building. One day Christ will be placed on God's building as the topstone. According to Zechariah 4:7, at that time all the people of God will shout, "Grace, grace to it."...Christ is the foundation stone, the cornerstone, and the topstone, not to be our supply but to be the very material for God's building. (*The Building of the Church*, pp. 49-50)

We need to experience all these aspects of Christ as the stone for God's building....This building is simply Christ Himself. The fact that Christ is the foundation stone is not a doctrine; it is something that we must experience. Apart from the church life, you cannot experience Christ as the foundation stone. Furthermore, outside the church life, it is impossible to experience Christ as the cornerstone, much less as the topstone. During the early days of the church life...you brothers probably did not have very much experience of Christ as the foundation stone. But after the stormy winds began to blow and attacks began to come upon the church, you realized that you cannot afford to be the church without a foundation. You had to experience Christ in such a way that you could withstand the storm and the tide. This is the experience of Christ as the foundation. Praise the Lord that...the foundation has been laid!

Gradually, after the laying of the foundation, you began to experience Christ as the cornerstone, as the One who joins the building together. It is not enough for the walls to be solid; they must also be connected. They are joined by your experience of Christ as the connecting element, that is, as the cornerstone. (*The Kernel of the Bible*, p. 110)

*Further Reading: The Kernel of the Bible*, ch. 11; *The Building of the Church*, chs. 3-4

*Enlightenment and inspiration:* _____

_____

_____

_____

## *Morning Nourishment*

**Psa. The stone which the builders rejected has become**
**118:22 the head of the corner.**
**Eph. In whom all the building, being fitted together, is**
**2:21 growing into a holy temple in the Lord.**

In Psalm 118 we have the thanksgiving of God's elect for God's bountiful goodness and everlasting lovingkindness leading to Christ as the cornerstone for God's building.

In verse 22a the psalmist speaks of "the stone which the builders rejected." Verse 26 indicates that the psalmist was referring not to himself but to someone else. In His interpretation of verses 22 and 23, the Lord Jesus revealed that He was the cornerstone rejected by the Jewish leaders as the builders of God, who, in a sense, were building something for God. Although Christ was the stone given to them by God, they rejected Him to such an extent that they put Him on the cross.

Psalm 118:22b tells us that the stone which the builders rejected has become "the head of the corner." The Hebrew for "head of the corner" can also be translated "chief cornerstone." Although Christ was rejected by Israel as the builders of God, in resurrection God made Him the cornerstone for God's building. In Isaiah 28:16 Christ is unveiled as the foundation stone; in Zechariah 4:7, as the topstone; and in Psalm 118:22, as the cornerstone. Of these three kinds of stones, the cornerstone is the most crucial, for it joins together the two walls and thus enables God's building to stand. (*Life-study of the Psalms,* pp. 444-445)

## *Today's Reading*

The stone is Christ, who is for God's building (Isa. 28:16; Zech. 3:9; 1 Pet. 2:4), and the builders are the Jewish leaders, who should have been working on God's building. (Matt. 21:42, footnote 1)

[In Ephesians 2:20] Christ is referred to not as the foundation (Isa. 28:16) but as the cornerstone, because the main concern here is not the foundation but the cornerstone that joins together the two walls, one wall being the Jewish believers, and the other, the Gentile believers. Here, not Christ but the apostles and prophets who received the revelation concerning Christ are stressed as the foundation. When the Jewish builders rejected Christ, they rejected Him as the cornerstone (Acts 4:11; 1 Pet. 2:7), the One who would join the Gentiles to them for the building of God's house. (Eph. 2:20, footnote 3)

In Christ, who is the cornerstone, all the building, including both the Jewish and the Gentile believers, is fitted together and is growing into a holy temple in the Lord. (Eph. 2:21, footnote 1)

First Peter 2:6 says, "Behold, I lay in Zion a cornerstone, chosen and precious; and he who believes on Him shall by no means be put to shame." Here we see that Christ is the chosen stone laid in Zion, the precious cornerstone, and that he who believes on Him shall by no means be put to shame. The expression *on Him* implies that Christ is a base, a standing. This indicates that Christ as the cornerstone is a base upon which we put our faith. We believe on this cornerstone as a strong base; hence, we will never be put to shame. Christ is trustworthy, stable, and steadfast. We can put our trust in Him and be assured that we will never be put to shame.

In God's New Testament economy Christ as the cornerstone, in His saving us (Acts 4:11-12), first makes us living stones for the building up of God's spiritual house (Matt. 16:16-18; John 1:42; 1 Pet. 2:2-6), and then, in the process of His transforming us (Rom. 12:2a; 2 Cor. 3:18), builds us up into a dwelling place of God (Eph. 2:19-22), that He may carry out God's eternal economy for God's good pleasure (1:9; 3:9-11).

As the all-inclusive stone, Christ is the centrality of God's move for the building up of His eternal habitation (Matt. 21:42, 44; Zech. 3:9, cf. Rev. 5:5-6; Acts 4:10-12; Isa. 28:16; Eph. 2:19-22; 1 Pet. 2:4-8; Dan. 2:34-35; Zech. 4:7; Rev. 21:11, cf. 4:3). Everything Christ is, everything He has done, and everything He is doing is due to the fact that He is the cornerstone. (*The Conclusion of the New Testament,* p. 3873)

*Further Reading: The Conclusion of the New Testament,* msgs. 59, 336, 383

## *Enlightenment and inspiration:* _____

_____

_____

_____

## *Morning Nourishment*

**1 Pet.** ..."Behold, I lay in Zion a cornerstone, chosen *and*
**2:6-7** precious; and he who believes on Him shall by no
means be put to shame." To you therefore who
believe is the preciousness; but to the unbelieving,
"The stone which the builders rejected, this has
become the head of the corner."
**Psa..** This is the day that Jehovah has made; let us exult
**118:24** and rejoice in it.

The Psalms unveil Christ to us in a complete way. If we did not
have Psalm 118, the revelation concerning Christ in the Psalms
would not have been completed. Christ is unveiled from Psalm 2
through Psalm 110, which is the highest revelation of Christ. Nevertheless, we still need to see from Psalm 118 that Christ is the
stone rejected by the builders but honored by God as the cornerstone.
If Christ were not the cornerstone, He could not have died for us
and for our sins, and He could not have died with us. If He were
not the cornerstone, He could do nothing. Everything He is, everything He has done, and everything He is doing is due to the fact
that He is the cornerstone. In Acts 4 we see that as the cornerstone He is the Savior, and in Ephesians 2 we see that as the cornerstone He is the building factor. (*Life-study of the Psalms*, p. 446)

## *Today's Reading*

In 1 Peter 2:4-7 we have another word about Christ as the cornerstone. "Coming to Him, a living stone, rejected by men but
with God chosen and precious, you yourselves also, as living
stones, are being built up as a spiritual house into a holy priesthood to offer up spiritual sacrifices acceptable to God through
Jesus Christ. For it is contained in Scripture: 'Behold, I lay in Zion
a cornerstone, chosen and precious; and he who believes on Him
shall by no means be put to shame.' To you therefore who believe
is the preciousness; but to the unbelieving, 'The stone which the
builders rejected, this has become the head of the corner.'" How
can we who are lifeless clay become living stones? We can become

living stones only through Christ's being the cornerstone. Christ as the cornerstone is the factor for many things. We have been saved because Christ is the cornerstone. Now we are being transformed and built up also because Christ is the cornerstone. (*Life-study of the Psalms*, p. 446)

God's intention in saving us is not to bring us into the heavens; rather, it is to join us to the Jews so that He may have His building. Many unbelieving Jews despise the Lord Jesus because they do not want to be joined to the Gentiles. As long as a Jew does not believe in Christ, he may be separated from the Gentiles. But as soon as such a Jew believes in Him, he is joined by Christ, the cornerstone, to the Gentile believers. Whether we are Jews or Gentiles, we have been saved in order to be joined together in Christ for God's building.... [In Ephesians 2:21] we see that in Christ, who is the cornerstone, all the building, including both Jewish and Gentile believers, is fitted together and is growing into a holy temple. (*Life-study of Ephesians*, pp. 235-236)

This day [in Psalm 118:24] is the day of Christ's resurrection. On the day of His resurrection the Lord Jesus was made the cornerstone by God. Christ was chosen by God in eternity past to be the cornerstone for God's spiritual building (1 Pet. 1:20; 2:4). Then, the Jewish leaders as the builders rejected Him to the uttermost, to such an extent that they put Him on the cross (Matt. 21:38-42a). God chose Christ as the cornerstone a second time in Christ's resurrection (Acts 4:10-11), thereby confirming His initial choosing of Christ in eternity past. After God resurrected Christ, He uplifted Him to the heavens (Luke 24:51; Acts 1:9). Christ's ascension to Zion in the heavens (Rev. 14:1) was a further confirmation that God had chosen Him to be the cornerstone (Isa. 28:16; 1 Pet. 2:6). Both Christ's resurrection and His ascension prove and confirm that He is the One whom God has chosen to be the head of the corner for God's building. (Psa. 118:24, footnote 1)

*Further Reading: Life-study of Ephesians, msg. 27; The Vision and Experience of the Corporate Christ, ch. 5.*

*Enlightenment and inspiration:* _____

_____

_____

### Morning Nourishment

1 Pet.   Coming to Him, a living stone, rejected by men but
2:4-5   with God chosen *and* precious, you yourselves also,
        as living stones, are being built up as a spiritual
        house into a holy priesthood to offer up spiritual
        sacrifices acceptable to God through Jesus Christ.
Psa.   O Jehovah, do save, we pray! O Jehovah, do send
118:25   prosperity, we pray!

In Matthew 16 Peter received a complete vision of Christ and
the church. We know this to be true because he later preached the
gospel in an astonishing way, declaring, "Jesus Christ the Nazarene, whom you crucified and whom God has raised from the
dead,...this is the stone which was considered as nothing by you,
the builders, which has become the head of the corner" (Acts 4:10-
11). Peter preached that Christ is not only the Savior but also the
cornerstone to connect the two walls of God's building. Christ as the
cornerstone was disowned by the Jews yet honored and treasured
by God because God's desire is not only to save us but also to regen-
erate and transform us into precious stones to build up the church.
(*The Vision and Experience of the Corporate Christ,* p. 47)

### Today's Reading

This revelation concerning Christ as the cornerstone is unveiled in the praises of the psalmist. Often, while the psalmists
were expressing their complex sentiments, something suddenly
came forth as a revelation concerning Christ....Have you ever
thanked the Lord for being the cornerstone or praised Him for
His being the cornerstone? I doubt that many among us have
done this. We need to pray, saying, "Lord Jesus, I thank You that
You are the cornerstone as my Savior and as my salvation. I
praise You that You are the cornerstone for God's building. Without You we do not have any element or factor to be built up as
God's temple."...I would encourage you to pray like this: "Lord, I
thank You for unveiling to me that You are the cornerstone to be
my salvation and to be the element and factor for me to be transformed and built up into Your habitation."

Psalm 118:23 says, "This is from Jehovah; / It is wonderful in our sight." Here we are told that Christ's becoming the cornerstone was from Jehovah and that it is wonderful in our eyes.... Verse 24a goes on to say, "This is the day that Jehovah has made." This day is the day of Christ's resurrection. On the day of His resurrection, on the Lord's Day (Acts 20:7; 1 Cor. 16:2; Rev. 1:10), the Lord Jesus was made the cornerstone by God. This is why we like to meet together on the Lord's Day, a very particular day....Psalm 118:24b continues, "Let us exult and rejoice in it." Here we are charged to exult and rejoice in this day. This indicates that we should come to the meetings with rejoicing, praising the Lord. However, when many come to the meetings, they are silent, as if they do not have a spirit and a mouth. In the meetings, let us exercise our spirit and open our mouth to rejoice in the Lord and to praise Him for His being made the cornerstone.

Verse 25 says, "O Jehovah, do save, we pray! / O Jehovah, do send prosperity, we pray!" In Hebrew the words "do save" are *hoshiah-na,* the source for *hosanna* in the New Testament (Matt. 21:9; Mark 11:9-10; John 12:13). The prosperity mentioned in Psalm 118:25 is not material; rather, it refers to rich blessings that are heavenly, spiritual, and divine. This is the kind of prosperity described in Ephesians 1, which speaks of the heavenly, spiritual, and divine blessings given to us by the Triune God. Verse 3 says, "Blessed be the God and Father of our Lord Jesus Christ, who has blessed us with every spiritual blessing in the heavenlies in Christ." According to Ephesians 1, the first portion of these blessings is of God the Father (vv. 3-6); the second portion is of God the Son (vv. 7-12); and the third portion is of God the Spirit (vv. 13-14). If we are interested in these blessings, we will be brought into the enjoyment of the prosperity sent to us by God because of Christ's being the cornerstone. (*Life-study of the Psalms,* pp. 447-449)

*Further Reading: Life-study of the Psalms,* msg. 39; *Christ and the Church Revealed and Typified in the Psalms,* ch. 20

## *Enlightenment and inspiration:* _____

_____

_____

_____

## *Morning Nourishment*

**Matt.** **And I also say to you that you are Peter, and upon**
**16:18** **this rock I will build My church, and the gates of**
**Hades shall not prevail against it.**
**21:42** **Jesus said to them, Have you never read in the**
**Scriptures, "The stone which the builders rejected,**
**this has become the head of the corner. This was**
**from the Lord, and it is marvelous in our eyes"?**

I am not interested in merely teaching you or edifying you. I
am doing my best to minister the element of Christ into you. I do
not like to pass on knowledge. Instead, I would minister the
transforming Christ into you. If you take this Christ into you,
you will never be the same....Hallelujah for the injections of
Christ! I have the full confidence that these heavenly injections
will make us stones for the church today and ultimately for the
New Jerusalem. (*The Kernel of the Bible,* p. 106)

## *Today's Reading*

Today, many people talk about Christ building the church....
If we would let Him build His church, we must learn to take such
a wonderful person as our life. We all have been put into such a
wonderful person, and now He has come into us that we may live
by Him. Only in this way will we have the life that is qualified for
the church building.

When Jesus said that He would build His church, He did not
say it in the second or third chapter of Matthew, but in the six-
teenth chapter. It was after He became the Nazarene, the ful-
filler of righteousness, the One who daily feeds on the Word of
God, the great light, the greater temple, the greater Jonah, and
the greater Solomon. After He had been revealed in such a way,
He said that He would build His church. May the Lord open our
eyes that we may see the reality in the Lord's recovery. It is not a
new way to meet together. It is the reality of taking Christ as
such a wonderful person.

In Matthew [21:42] we see that Jesus was rejected not as the
Savior or Redeemer, but as the building stone....Many Christians

think that Jesus was rejected by the Jewish people as the Savior and Redeemer. But Jesus tells us that He was rejected not as the Redeemer, but as the cornerstone for God's building. His main purpose was not merely to be the Redeemer, but to be the cornerstone for building up God's house. The whole book of Matthew is for this purpose. He said that He would build His church, but the religious ones rejected Him as the cornerstone for God's building. Therefore, they could never be a part of the building of God, for they rejected the cornerstone....But, Hallelujah, we accept Him! We not only accept Him as the Savior and Redeemer, but also as the cornerstone. (*The Wonderful Christ in the Canon of the New Testament,* pp. 46-47)

In the constitution of the kingdom of the heavens [in Matthew 5—7] we cannot see what the will of the Father actually is. However, it is clearly revealed in chapter sixteen. The Father's will is to build the church upon the Son as the rock. This is fully developed in the Acts, the Epistles, and the book of Revelation. The New Testament reveals that God's divine, eternal will is to build up the church. (*Life-study of Matthew,* p. 303)

As the stone for God's building, Christ is not only the foundation, the corner, and the top, but also the One who is increasing and producing. He has produced us, and now He is increasing within us to make us living stones for God's building (1 Pet. 2:5).

In God's building everything is Christ. God's temple, God's eternal habitation, is Christ. In this building Christ is the foundation stone, the cornerstone, the topstone, and the living stone for the increase. At the bottom, at the top, on every side, and in every corner, we have Christ. Eventually, this Christ is the church. The church is the building with Christ as the foundation, the cornerstone, the topstone, the increasing wall, and ultimately as the entire building. This is the kernel of the Bible, Christ and the church. (*The Kernel of the Bible,* pp. 109-110)

*Further Reading: The Wonderful Christ in the Canon of the New Testament, ch. 4; Life-study of Acts, msg. 16*

## *Enlightenment and inspiration:* _____

_____

_____

_____

## *Morning Nourishment*

**Matt.** **You are the light of the world. It is impossible for a**
**5:14** **city situated upon a mountain to be hidden.**
**Psa.** **Blessed is He who comes in the name of Jehovah;**
**118:26** **we bless you from the house of Jehovah.**

In Matthew 5:14-16 we see that the kingdom is expressed in its shining as the light. In verse 14a...we see that the people of the kingdom of the heavens live a kingdom life to shine in the darkness of the world. The world, Satan's system, the dark human society, needs light. To the darkened world, the people of the kingdom of the heavens are a light effacing its darkness....In 5:14b the Lord Jesus goes on to say, "It is impossible for a city situated upon a mountain to be hidden." As the shining light, the kingdom people are like a city situated upon a mountain. Such a city cannot be hidden. Ultimately, this city will be consummated in the holy city of the New Jerusalem (Rev. 21:10-11, 23-24). (*The Conclusion of the New Testament*, p. 2659)

## *Today's Reading*

The light in Matthew 5:14 is not an individual person; on the contrary, it is a corporate city. This indicates that the kingdom people need the building. If we are in the building of the church in a practical way, we shall realize that only by being built together can we be a city situated upon a mountain. This city becomes a shining light. If the saints in the church in your locality are not built up but instead are scattered, divided, and separated, there is no city there. And as long as there is no city, there is no light, because the city is the light. The light is not an individual believer; it is a corporate city built up as one entity to shine over the people surrounding it. In order to shine upon others, we need to be built up as a city upon the mountaintop. For this, we need to keep the oneness and remain one entity, a corporate Body. Then we shall be a shining light as the expression of the kingdom. (*The Conclusion of the New Testament*, pp. 2659-2660)

Psalms 118:26a declares, "Blessed is He who comes in the name of Jehovah." This indicates that Christ will come in the name of God, in the name of Jehovah. In fact, He will come two times in the name of Jehovah....The first time is mentioned in Matthew 21:5-11. That was the time when Christ was warmly welcomed by the people in Jerusalem who said, "Blessed is He who comes in the name of the Lord!" (v. 9)....After Christ came in the name of Jehovah the first time, He was rejected by the Jews, and today they still will not welcome Him. However, when He comes back, the Jews will give Him a warm welcome and say, "Blessed is He who comes in the name of the Lord" (Matt. 23:39).

The Lord Jesus quoted Psalm 118 in Matthew 21:42 and in 23:39, each time applying the words of the psalm to Himself and thereby interpreting them. Without His interpretation, we could not understand that the cornerstone in Psalm 118:22 refers to Christ and that the word in verse 26 about "He who comes in the name of Jehovah" also refers to Christ. (*Life-study of the Psalms*, p. 449)

At the end of the war of Armageddon, Christ will come to earth, and the remnant of Israel will look on Him whom they have pierced (John 19:34, 37; Rev. 1:7), will repent and wail, and will believe in Christ and receive Him. In this way all Israel will be saved (Rom. 11:26-27). This will be the household salvation rendered to Israel by God. (Zech. 12:10, footnote 2)

Repentant Israel will wail over Christ as the only Son of God (John 1:18; 3:16) and will cry bitterly over Him as the firstborn Son of God (Rom. 8:29; Heb. 1:6a). Christ's being the only begotten Son is for us to be redeemed and to receive eternal life (John 3:14-16). Christ's becoming the firstborn Son through His death and resurrection (Rom. 1:3-4) is for us to become sons of God as heirs to inherit all the riches of what God is, that is, to receive, participate in, and enjoy all the riches of the Triune God (Rom. 8:14-17; Gal. 3:26, 29). In their repentance Israel will realize that as the only begotten Son Christ has redeemed them and has brought them eternal life and that as the firstborn Son He has made them heirs to inherit the riches of the Triune God as their enjoyment. (Zech. 12:10, footnote 5)

*Further Reading: The Conclusion of the New Testament*, msg. 253; *Life-study of Isaiah*, msg. 43; *Life-study of Zechariah*, msg. 13

### *Enlightenment and inspiration:* _____

_____
_____
_____

## *Hymns, #199*

1 Thou art the Rock everlasting,
   Spiritual Rock cleft for me;
Drinking of Thee as the Spirit,
   Thus I become one with Thee.
Thou art the Rock never shaken,
   'Tis on this Rock we are built;
Joined unto Thee thru redemption,
   Nothing can shake us thru guilt.

   Lord, how we treasure Thy value,
     All that Thou art is for us;
   While here in loving remembrance
     We share Thy wealth glorious.

2 Thou art the Stone tried by many,
   Precious to God, dear to us,
Thou art so sure and trustworthy,
   Thy strength is so marvelous.
Thou art the Stone that is living,
   Chosen of God, made our own;
So energetic and pow'rful,
   With endless life to us known.

3 Thou art the Stone of Foundation
   Laid by our God, safe and sure;
It is by this sure foundation
   Safety fore'er we secure.
To us no other foundation
   Of any kind man can lay;
Thou art the only foundation
   Which we have now and for aye.

4 Lord, for God's spiritual building,
   Thou art the Chief Cornerstone;
Both of the Jews and the Gentiles
   By Thee are built into one.
Lord, Thou art also the Topstone,
   Brought forth in measureless grace;
Thou art our cover and glory,
   Moving our hearts in Thy praise.

*[handwritten marginal notes:]*
Cleft rock
Eternal rock
Precious stone
living stone
Foundation stone
Cornerstone
Topstone

*Composition for prophecy with main point and sub-points:* _____

_____

_____

_____

_____

_____

_____

_____

_____

_____

_____

_____

_____

_____

_____

_____

_____

_____

_____

_____

_____

_____

_____

_____

_____

_____

_____

_____

_____

_____

_____

_____

_____

_____

_____

### The Functions and Blessings
### of God's Law as His Living Word
### to His Loving Seekers

Scripture Reading: Psa. 119

*Day 1*   **I. In Psalm 119 Christ is the reality of the law:**

A. Christ is the reality of the law as the testimony of God, the expression of God; the testimony of God signifies Christ, the embodiment of God (Col. 2:9), as the living portrait of what God is.

B. Christ is the reality of the law as the word of God, signifying Christ as the living Word of God breathed out by Him (Rev. 19:13b; 2 Tim. 3:16-17):

1. The written words are the letters, but the living Word is the Spirit, who is the reality of the letters (John 6:63; Eph. 6:17).

2. The law is the person of Christ, and the person of Christ is the Spirit (1 Cor. 15:45b; 2 Cor. 3:17).

3. The Spirit is the reality of whatever God is (John 16:13; 1 John 5:6); hence, as the Spirit, Christ is the reality of the law.

*Day 2*   **II. There are two aspects of the law—the aspect of the letter and the aspect of the Spirit as the reality of God's blessings (2 Cor. 3:6; Eph. 1:3):**

A. If our attitude in coming to the law is to care for the commandments in letters, we will have the law in the aspect of the killing letter.

B. However, if we take every part of the law—all the commandments, ordinances, statutes, precepts, and judgments—as the word breathed out by the God whom we love, we will have the law in the aspect of the life-giving Spirit.

**III. There are two aspects of the function of the law:**

A. The law has a negative aspect:

1. As God's commandments, the law exposes man's sin and subdues sinners before God (Rom. 7:7b; 3:19-20; 5:20a; 4:15b).

2. As God's regulations with statutes, ordinances, and rituals, the law functioned to guard God's chosen people in its custody that they might be conducted to Christ (Gal. 3:23-24).

B. The law has a positive aspect:

1. As God's living word, the law functions to minister the living God to His seekers (Psa. 119:2, 88).

2. As God's living word, the law functions to dispense God Himself as life and light into those who love the law (vv. 25, 50, 107, 116, 130, 154).

*Day 3*

3. As God's living word, the law functions to restore man's soul and make man's heart joyous (19:7-8).

4. As God's living word, the law functions to bring us salvation (119:41, 170).

5. As God's living word, the law functions to strengthen (v. 28), comfort (v. 76), and nourish us (v. 103).

6. As God's living word, the law functions to uphold us, keep us safe, and cause us to hope (vv. 116-117, 49).

7. As God's living word, the law causes us to enjoy God as our portion (v. 57).

8. As God's living word, the law causes us to enjoy God's countenance (v. 58) and the shining of His face (v. 135).

9. As God's living word, the law causes us to enjoy God as our hiding place and shield (v. 114) and also enjoy God's help and well-dealing (vv. 175, 65).

10. As God's living word, the law functions to make us wise and give us understanding (vv. 98-99).

11. As God's living word, the law functions to give us proper discernment and knowledge (v. 66).

12. As God's living word, the law functions to keep us from sinning and from every evil way (vv. 11, 101).

13. As God's living word, the law keeps us from stumbling (v. 165), establishes our footsteps, and causes us to overcome iniquity (v. 133).

*Day 4*

C. Whether in our experience the law is positive or negative depends on the condition of our heart in receiving the law:

1. If we love God, humble ourselves, and regard the law as His living word through which we contact Him and abide in Him, the law will become a channel through which the divine life and substance are conveyed to us for our supply and nourishment; being infused with God's substance through the law as God's word, we will become one with God in life, nature, and expression and will spontaneously live a life that expresses God and corresponds to His law (Rom. 8:4; Phil. 1:21a).

2. However, if in coming to the law we do not seek God in love but rather separate the law from the living God as the source of life, the law, which was intended to result in life but cannot give life of itself, will become a condemning and killing element to us (Exo. 19:8; John 5:39-40; Rom. 7:10-11; Gal. 3:21; 2 Cor. 3:6-7, 9; cf. Exo. 23:19b and footnote 2).

*Day 5* **IV. There are two kinds of people in relation to the law:**

A. The first kind is the letter-keepers, illustrated by the Judaizers and Saul of Tarsus (Phil. 3:6b, 2).

B. The second kind is the God-seekers, illustrated by the psalmists, especially by the writer of Psalm 119, and by the apostle Paul (2 Cor. 3:6):

1. They seek God with all their heart (Psa. 119:2).

2. They love God's name and remember it (vv. 132, 55).

3. They entreat God's face (v. 58).

4. They ask for God's face to shine on them (v. 135).

5. They walk in God's presence (v. 168).

6. They consider God's law to be God's word (vv. 17-18, 28-29).

7. God's word is sweeter than honey to their mouth (v. 103).

8. God's word is more precious than fine gold to them (v. 127).

    9. God's word is a lamp to their feet and a light to their path (vv. 105, 130).

V. **Psalm 119 expresses the attitude of God's loving seekers toward God's law as His living word:**

A. They choose God's word (vv. 30, 173).

B. They believe God's word (v. 66).

*Day 6*

C. They lift up their hand to God's word, indicating that they receive the word of God warmly and gladly and say Amen to it (v. 48a; Neh. 8:5-6).

D. They love God's word (Psa. 119:47-48, 97, 113, 119, 127, 140, 159, 163, 165, 167).

E. They delight in God's word (vv. 16, 24, 35, 47, 70, 77, 92, 174).

F. They taste God's word (v. 103).

G. They rejoice in God's word (vv. 14, 111, 162).

H. They sing God's word (v. 54).

I. They regard God's word (vv. 6, 117).

J. They have a perfect heart in God's word (v. 80).

K. They incline their heart to God's word (vv. 36, 112).

L. They seek God's word (vv. 45, 94), long for it (vv. 20, 40, 131), and hope in it with prayer (vv. 43, 74, 114, 147).

M. They trust in God's word (v. 42).

N. They muse on God's word (vv. 15, 23, 48, 78, 99, 148):

    1. Rich in meaning, the Hebrew word for *muse* implies to worship, to converse with oneself, and to speak aloud; to muse on the word is to taste and enjoy it through careful considering.

    2. Prayer, speaking to oneself, and praising the Lord may also be included in musing on the word; to muse on the word of God is to enjoy His word as His breath (2 Tim. 3:16) and thus to be infused with God, to breathe God in, and to receive spiritual nourishment.

O. They consider God's word (Psa. 119:95b).

P. They esteem God's word to be right in all things (v. 128a).

Q. They learn God's word (vv. 73, 71).

R.  They treasure God's word (vv. 14, 162, 72, 127, 111).

S.  They treasure up God's word in their heart (v. 11).

T.  They remember God's word and do not forget it (vv. 52, 16b, 93).

U.  They stand in awe of God's word (vv. 161b, 120).

V.  They cling to God's word (v. 31).

W.  They do not forsake God's word, do not swerve from it, do not turn aside from it, and do not stray from it (vv. 87, 51, 157, 102, 110).

X.  They turn their feet toward God's word (v. 59).

Y.  They keep, observe, and do God's word (vv. 33, 69).

Z.  They walk in God's word and run the way of God's word (vv. 1, 32a).

## Morning Nourishment

Exo. **And he was there with Jehovah forty days and**
34:28 **forty nights; he did not eat bread, and he did not**
**drink water. And He wrote upon the tablets the**
**words of the covenant, the Ten Commandments.**
2 Tim. **All Scripture is God-breathed and profitable for**
3:16-17 **teaching, for conviction, for correction, for instruc-**
**tion in righteousness, that the man of God may be**
**complete, fully equipped for every good work.**
Rev. **...His name is called the Word of God.**
19:13

In both the Old Testament and the New Testament there is a strong basis for saying that the law in its reality is Christ. If we would see that Christ is the reality of the law, we need to regard the law, as Psalm 119 does, as the testimony of God and as the word of God. This psalm does not contain the word "Christ," but it does contain a number of synonyms of Christ, such as "testimony" and "word," which are also synonyms of "law." We should not consider the law merely as commandments, regulations, and ordinances. Rather, we should consider the law as God's testimony. The law was given on Mount Sinai, but it was put into a little ark called "the Ark of the Testimony" (Exo. 25:16). The Ark was then placed into "the Tabernacle of the Testimony" (38:21). Thus, the law was in the Ark of the Testimony, and the Ark of the Testimony was in the Tabernacle of the Testimony.

The Ten Commandments are not a person, but they are a portrait of a person. A law is always a picture of the person who makes it. The laws passed by today's legislators are pictures of the legislators. The principle is the same with the law of God. The law of God—the Ten Commandments with the many statutes, ordinances, and judgments—is a portrait of the person of God. (*Life-study of the Psalms,* pp. 451-452)

## Today's Reading

Christ is the reality of the law as the testimony of God. The testimony of God signifies Christ as the living portrait of what God is (Col. 2:9; 1:19).

The Ten Commandments are brief, but they give us a portrait of God. They show us that God is a jealous God, that He cannot tolerate other gods. In this matter, He is like a husband who is jealous concerning his wife. Also, God is a God of love, light, holiness, and righteousness. Here we have five crucial words—jealous, love, light, holiness, and righteousness.

Christ is the reality of the law not only as the testimony of God but also as the word of God, signifying Christ as the living word of God breathed out by Him (Rev. 19:13b; 2 Tim. 3:16-17). John 1:1 says that in the beginning was the Word (Christ), that the Word was with God, and that the Word was God. According to Revelation 19:13b, when Christ comes back to judge, His name will be called "the Word of God." The Ten Commandments, with all their statutes, ordinances, and judgments, are also called the word of God. A literal rendering of the Hebrew translated "Ten Commandments" in Exodus 34:28 would be "ten words." The Ten Commandments are thus God's words, breathed out by Him.

Psalm 119 is a psalm of one hundred seventy-six verses describing Christ, who is the reality of the law, the commandments, the ordinances, the statutes, the precepts, and the judgments. In total, He is the Word of God. The words of Psalm 119 are the written words of God, but Christ is the living Word of God. The written words are the letters, but the living Word is the Spirit, who is the reality of the letters.

Now we can see not only what the law is but also who the law is. Who is the law? The law is the person of Christ, and the person of Christ is the Spirit. The Spirit is the reality of whatever God is. Hence, as the Spirit, Christ is the reality of the law. Eventually, this law, this person, consummates in the way (John 14:6). When we have Him, we have not only love and light but also the way. This is Christ being the reality of the law as the testimony and the word of God. (*Life-study of the Psalms,* pp. 452-454)

*Further Reading: Life-study of Exodus,* msg. 51

*__Enlightenment and inspiration:__* _____

_____
_____
_____

## Morning Nourishment

2 Cor. Who has also made us sufficient as ministers of a
3:6 new covenant, *ministers* not of the letter but of the
Spirit; for the letter kills, but the Spirit gives life.
Psa. ...I love Your commandments more than gold, indeed,
119:127 more than fine gold.
130 The opening of Your words gives light, imparting
understanding to the simple.

There are two aspects of the law—the aspect of the letter and
the aspect of the Spirit [2 Cor. 3:6]....Whether you have a killing
law or a life-giving law depends on your attitude. If your attitude
in coming to the law is to care only for the commandments in letters and to realize that you cannot fulfill these commandments,
then you have the law in the aspect of the letter. However, if you
take every part of the law—all the commandments, ordinances,
statutes, precepts, and judgments—as the word breathed out by
the God whom you love, then you will have the law in the aspect
of the Spirit. Then instead of trembling before the law of letters,
you will be happy to be fed with every part of the law as the word,
the breath, of God. (*Life-study of the Psalms,* pp. 454-455)

## Today's Reading

Just as the law itself has two aspects, so also the function of the
law has two aspects [—a negative aspect and a positive aspect].

[In its negative aspect] as God's commandments, the law
exposes man's sin (Rom. 7:7b; 3:20b; 5:20a; 4:15b). Every item of
the law with its statutes and ordinances exposes our shortcom-
ings, defects, dishonesty, and unfaithfulness. For example, the
commandment about not worshipping idols may expose the fact
that many things are idols to us. For some people a pen or a dia-
mond is an idol. Also, the commandment about keeping the Sabbath may expose our not resting regularly according to God's
ordination. By failing to rest properly we fail to enjoy God's love
expressed in the commandment to keep the Sabbath.

As God's regulations with statutes, ordinances, and rituals,
the law functioned to guard God's chosen people in its custody

that they might be conducted to Christ (Gal. 3:23-24). The law kept God's chosen people in custody, in ward, in the proper way until Christ came. The sheepfold in John 10 signifies the custody of the law. The Lord Jesus is the door of the sheepfold (v. 9), and through Him all those who were in the sheepfold could come out. Thus, on the negative side the law functioned to [expose man's sin] and to guard God's chosen people until Christ came.

[Positively], as God's living testimony, the law functions to minister the living God to His seekers (Psa. 119:2, 88)....If we regard the law as God's testimony, as a portrait of God, and if we consider that every word of the law is something breathed out by God, then to us the law will be the living and loving word of God. If this is our attitude toward the Bible today, then whenever we come to the Bible, we will have the sense deep within that we are with God. Then as we read the Bible, we will touch God, knowing that He is loving and that it is surely worthwhile for us to love Him and to seek Him. This is the positive function of the law as the testimony of God.

As God's living word the law functions to dispense God's life and light into those who love the law (vv. 25, 116, 130). We all should regard the Bible as the living word of God which dispenses God Himself into us as our life and light. Whether or not this is our experience depends upon whether we seek God and love Him. This means that what the Bible is to us depends upon our attitude toward the Bible. (*Life-study of the Psalms,* pp. 455-456)

In Psalms 119 and 19 we see at least twenty-six functions of God's law as His living word to those who lovingly seek Him.... The Word of God gives us light. It also gives life (119:25, 50, 107, 154). If you read Psalm 119 carefully, you will notice that the word enliven is used a number of times....The Word of God gives us light; then it quickens us, enlivens us, gives us life. Therefore, we live by the living Word; that is, we live by God Himself. (*Life-study of Exodus,* p. 686)

*Further Reading: Life-study of the Psalms,* msg. 40; *Life-study of Exodus,* msg. 58

### *Enlightenment and inspiration:* _____

_____

_____

_____

## *Morning Nourishment*

Psa. **The law of Jehovah is perfect, restoring the soul;**
19:7-8 **the testimony of Jehovah is faithful, making the**
**simple wise; the precepts of Jehovah are right,**
**making the heart joyous; the commandment of**
**Jehovah is clear, enlightening the eyes.**
119:25 **...Enliven me according to Your word.**
103 **How sweet are Your words to my taste!** *Sweeter*
**than honey to my mouth!**

Another function of the Word of God is to restore man's soul
and rejoice man's heart (Psa. 19:7-8). We need to be not only
quickened by the Word, but also restored by it, especially when
we are depressed, suppressed, or oppressed. After working all
day at your job, you may be under the oppression of Satan and
may be in need of restoration. On your way home from work,
take time to read, pray, and sing the Word. You will find that the
Word will restore your soul and cause your heart to rejoice.

The Word of God also brings us salvation (Psa. 119:41, 170).
We need salvation every day, even every moment. The living
Word of God brings us God's instant and constant salvation.
(*Life-study of Exodus*, p. 686)

## *Today's Reading*

The Word of God strengthens us (Psa. 119:28), comforts us
(v. 76), and nourishes us (v. 103). The psalmist said that God's
word was sweet to his taste, sweeter than honey to his mouth.
This indicates that he was nourished by the Word.

As the Word of God nourishes us, it upholds us. The Word
holds us up. It also keeps us safe and causes us to hope (vv. 116-
117, 49). When we experience the function of the living Word, we
shall not be without hope. Rather, we shall be hopeful in all
things. In Philippians 1:20 Paul could speak of his earnest
expectation and hope.

The Word of God also causes us to enjoy God as our portion
(Psa. 119:57). If we would enjoy Christ as our portion in the
Word, we should not only study the Word, but receive the Word

in a living way by praying, singing, psalming, and thanking.

Through the Word we enjoy God's countenance (v. 58) and the shining of His face (v. 135). While the children of Israel were in fear and trembling at the foot of Mount Sinai, Moses was on the mountaintop enjoying the shining of the Lord's countenance. Our situation should be that of Moses on the mountaintop, not that of the children of Israel at the foot of the mountain. We should be on the mountaintop under the shining of the face of God.

Through the Word we may enjoy God as our hiding place and shield (v. 114) and also enjoy God's help and well-dealing (vv. 175, 65). In every way God deals well with us. His care is comprehensive; He meets our every need. Even His rebuke is an aspect of His well-dealing. If we get into His Word in a living way, we shall enjoy His well-dealing.

Psalm 119:98 says, "Your commandments make me wiser than my enemies," and verse 99 says, "I have more insight than all my teachers, / For Your testimonies are my musing." These verses indicate that the Word of God makes us wise. The more we get into the Word, the wiser we become.

The Word of God also gives us proper discernment and knowledge (v. 66). Many Christians today are short of discernment. They are like those who cannot discern between their thumb and their fingers. We need to be very discerning. The Word of God gives us the needed discernment and knowledge.

Verse 11 says, "In my heart I have treasured up Your word / That I might not sin against You." According to this verse, the Word of God keeps us from sinning. The Word also keeps our feet from every evil way (v. 101).

The Word of God also keeps us from stumbling (v. 165), establishes our footsteps, and causes us to overcome iniquity (v. 133). No iniquity will have dominion over us. Instead, we shall conquer all evil things, for the Word of God will make us conquerors, overcomers. (*Life-study of Exodus,* pp. 686-688)

*Further Reading: Life-study of Exodus,* msgs. 51, 57

### *Enlightenment and inspiration:* _____

_____

_____

_____

## Morning Nourishment

**Rom. That the righteous requirement of the law might
8:4 be fulfilled in us, who do not walk according to the
flesh but according to the spirit.**

**Exo. ...You shall not boil a kid in its mother's milk.
23:19**

[The law is] not consciously kept by us through our outward endeavoring but [is] spontaneously and unconsciously fulfilled in us by the inward working of the Spirit of life. The Spirit of life is the Spirit of Christ, and Christ corresponds with the law of God. This Spirit within us spontaneously fulfills all the righteous requirements of the law through us when we walk according to Him. (Rom. 8:4, footnote 1)

Exodus 23:19 typifies that the milk of the word of God, the life supply of Christ, should be used to nourish new believers in Christ (1 Pet. 2:2; Heb. 5:12-13; 1 Cor. 3:2) and not to "kill" them (2 Cor. 3:6—"the letter kills"). (Exo. 23:19, footnote 2)

In 2 Corinthians 3:6 Paul says that the letter kills. Whether the law kills us or supplies us with life depends on how we deal with it. If we regard the law as the living word of God through which we contact the Lord and abide with Him, the law will become a channel for the supply of life. The source of life is the Lord Himself. The law in itself is not such a source, but it is a channel through which the divine life and substance are conveyed to us for supply and nourishment. What a blessing it is to receive the law in this way! (*Life-study of Exodus,* pp. 666-667)

## Today's Reading

The law is...the living word of God which infuses God's substance into those who lovingly seek Him. If we consider the Ten Commandments only as laws and then try to keep them, we are not proper in our approach to the law....On the contrary, we should be those who love God and seek Him. In this matter, we should be like Paul in Philippians 3, one who was pursuing Christ out of love and even running after Him. Out of love for the Lord, we should pursue Him, contact Him, and abide in His presence, dwelling together with Him. If we do this, day by day we shall be infused with God. Then automatically we shall walk according to God's law. We shall keep the requirements of the law, not by our own efforts, but with what has been infused into us of the Lord through our contact with Him. Once we have been thoroughly infused with God's substance, He Himself from within us will keep His own law. We should remember that the law was given on the mountain of God, the place where God's people could be infused with His substance. Thus, we should not regard the law simply as His commandments, but as the word of God and the testimony of God, which not only express Him, but also infuse His substance into those who seek Him in love.

If our condition is normal, we should be helped and very much blessed whenever we come to the Word of God....All Scripture is God-breathed (2 Tim. 3:16); therefore, the words of the Bible are God's breath. Furthermore, as the embodiment of God (Col. 2:9), the Lord Jesus is Himself called the Word (John 1:1, 14; Rev. 19:13). Thus, coming to the Word should be the equivalent of coming to God. Because the Word is the embodiment of God, it contains the riches of God. The Word of God contains all that God is. This is the reason the Word of God is so rich, substantial, living, and enlightening....The Bible requires more of us than any other book. The Bible demands that we humble ourselves and put aside our self-confidence and self-assurance....Let us learn to pray, "Lord, have mercy on me. I don't want to be covered by anything, and I don't want to have anything between You and me. Lord, grant that there will be nothing between us." This should be not only our prayer, but also our attitude toward the Lord.

Whether or not the Bible is shining in our experience depends on our attitude and condition. If we are humble and ask the Lord for mercy, the Bible will be to us a book of light. After reading a portion of the Word, you may not have much understanding, but you have the sense that you are in light. (*Life-study of Exodus,* pp. 607-608, 690, 693-694, 696)

*Further Reading: Life-study of Exodus,* msgs. 52, 56, 59

***Enlightenment and inspiration:*** _____

_____
_____
_____

## Morning Nourishment

Psalm   **Deal bountifully with Your servant that I may live**
119:17-18 **and keep Your word. Open my eyes that I may**
        **behold wondrous things out of Your law.**
  105   **Your word is a lamp to my feet and a light to my path.**
  127   **Therefore I love Your commandments more than**
        **gold, indeed, more than fine gold.**

There are two kinds of people in relation to the law....The first
kind is the letter-keepers, illustrated by the Judaizers and Saul of
Tarsus (Phil. 3:6b). The Judaizers, who were zealous for Judaism,
were a damage to the Lord Jesus in the Gospels, to the apostles in
the Acts, and to the believers in the Epistles. Paul, before he was
saved, was a strong Judaizer. In Philippians 3:2 Paul referred to
the Judaizers as "dogs" and "evil workers," saying, "Beware of the
dogs, beware of the evil workers, beware of the concision."...The
second kind is the God-seekers, illustrated by the psalmists, especially by the writer of Psalm 119. (*Life-study of the Psalms,* pp. 456-457)

## Today's Reading

"Blessed are those who keep His testimonies, / Who seek Him
with all their heart" (Psa. 119:2). The writer of this psalm was
one who sought God with his whole heart.

Verse 132 says, "Turn to me, and be gracious to me, / As is Your
custom with those who love Your name." This verse indicates that
the psalmist loved God's name. Verse 55 says, "I have remembered Your name / In the night, O Jehovah, / And have kept Your
law." When the psalmist awoke during the night, he remembered
God's name. May we all love God's name and remember it.

The psalmist also entreated God's countenance (v. 58). To
seek a person's countenance, his face, is actually to seek his
favor. If we seek God's countenance, we will receive bounty.
Often little children will earnestly seek the face of their mother.
To them nothing is more precious than beholding the face of
their mother. We also should seek God in such an intimate way.
If we seek God in this way, we will not regard the law as letters
but as a portrait of God which bears His countenance.

"Cause Your face to shine on Your servant, / And teach me Your statutes" (v. 135). Here we see that the psalmist lovingly sought God in an intimate way, even asking Him to cause His face to shine upon him.

"I have kept Your precepts and Your testimonies, / For all my ways are before You" (v. 168). This indicates that the psalmist walked in God's presence.

Verses 17 and 18...[indicate] that the psalmist considered God's law to be His word. This is indicated also by what the psalmist says in verses 28 and 29: "My soul melts because of grief; / Strengthen me according to Your word. / Remove from me the way of falsehood, / And graciously grant me Your law." These verses prove that the psalmist thought of God's law as His living and loving word breathed out of God's mouth.

For the psalmists God's word was sweeter than honey to their mouth (v. 103).

[Verse 127] indicates that to the psalmists God's word was more precious than fine gold.

God's word was a lamp to the psalmists' feet and a light to their path (v. 105).

In Psalm 119 many different verbs are used to express the attitude of the God-seekers toward God's law as God's testimony and God's word.

Psalm 119:30 says, "I have chosen the way of faithfulness; / Your ordinances I have set before me." Verse 173 says, "Let Your hand be ready to help me, / For I have chosen Your precepts." Like the psalmists, we all should choose God's word, making a strong decision in favor of the word of God.

Considering God's law to be His word, the psalmist believed in the word. Verse 66 says, "Teach me proper discernment and knowledge, / For I believe in Your commandments." We all must believe in the genuineness, accuracy, authority, and power of God's word. (*Life-study of the Psalms,* pp. 457-459)

*Further Reading: Life-study of the Psalms,* msg. 40

### *Enlightenment and inspiration:* _____

_____

_____

_____

## *Morning Nourishment*

**Psa.** And I will lift up my hand to Your commandments,
**119:48** which I love; and I will muse upon Your statutes.
**147-148** I anticipated the dawn and cried out; I hoped in
Your words. My eyes anticipated the night watches,
that I might muse upon Your word.
**162** I rejoice at Your word, like one who finds great spoil.

To lift up our hand to God's word is to welcome it [Psa.
119:48a]. Therefore, to lift up our hand unto the word of God is to
indicate that we receive it warmly and gladly and that we say
"amen" to it....Many times the writer of this psalm declared that
he loves God's word (vv. 47, 48, 97, 113, 119, 127, 140, 159, 163,
165, 167). We all should be able to testify that we love the word of
God....The psalmist also delighted in God's word (vv. 16, 24, 35,
47, 70, 77, 92, 174). He enjoyed the word of God and found it a
source of delight. Every day we should have a time to delight
ourselves in the Word.

To the psalmist the law was not merely a list of commandments; it was also a word full of enjoyment and life supply. For
this reason, God's words were sweet to his taste [v. 103]. If we
regard the law as nothing more than the commandments of
God, it will not be sweet to us. But if we regard God's law as His
word for our nourishment and life supply, we will enjoy its sweet
taste....When we taste the word of God, we rejoice in it. This was
the experience of the psalmist, who testified again and again
that he rejoiced in God's word (vv. 14, 111, 162). (*Life-study of the
Psalms*, pp. 459-460)

## *Today's Reading*

In Psalm 119:36 the psalmist prayed, "Incline my heart to Your
testimonies / And not to unjust gain." Then in verse 112 he declared, "I have inclined my heart to perform Your statutes / Forever,
to the end." These verses show us that we need a heart inclined to
the word of God. Sometimes as we are reading the Bible, our heart
is inclined to something else. Because our heart has the tendency
to depart from God's word, we need to pray that our heart will be

called back to God's word and be inclined to it....The psalmist also sought God's word (vv. 45, 94), longed for it (vv. 20, 40, 131), and hoped in it with prayer (vv. 43, 74, 114, 147)....In verse 42 the psalmist declared that he trusted in God's word.

In several verses the writer of Psalm 119 tells us that he mused upon God's word (vv. 15, 23, 48, 78, 99, 148). To muse on the word is to taste it through careful considering. Thus, musing is a kind of enjoyment. I can testify that most of the enlightenment I receive comes by musing on the Word early in the morning. As I muse on the Word, I think about it with much consideration in a detailed way....In verse 95b the psalmist said, "I consider Your testimonies." To consider the Word is to think it over very carefully. Concerning this, we may use the word *mull*. To consider the Word is to mull it over, even to study it and research it.

The psalmist also treasured the word of God. He treasured it as much as all riches (v. 14), as great spoil (v. 162), better than gold and silver (vv. 72, 127), and as a heritage forever (v. 111)....In verse 11 we are told that the psalmist treasured up God's word in his heart. Paul charged us to let the word of Christ dwell in us richly (Col. 3:16). We should not only memorize the word and keep it within us—we should treasure it up in our heart....In Psalm 119:52 the psalmist indicates that he remembered God's word. If we treasure up the word in our heart, we will remember it; we will call back, or recall, our enjoyment of it. In...verse 93 [the writer] said, "I will never forget Your precepts, / For by them You have enlivened me."

In verse 31 the psalmist said to God, "I cling to Your testimonies." We also need to cling to the word of God....Furthermore, the psalmist said that he did not forsake God's word, did not swerve from it, did not turn aside from it, and did not go astray from it (vv. 87, 51, 157, 102, 110)...."I considered my ways / And turned my feet toward Your testimonies" (v. 59). Instead of turning aside from the law, we, like the psalmist, should turn our feet toward it. (*Life-study of the Psalms,* pp. 460-463)

*Further Reading: Life-study of Exodus,* msg. 60

### *Enlightenment and inspiration:* _____

_____

_____

_____

## *Hymns,* #811

1   My heart is hungry, my spirit doth thirst;
    I come to Thee, Lord, to seek Thy supply;
    All that I need is none other but Thee,
    Thou canst my hunger and thirst satisfy.

      Feed me, Lord Jesus, give me to drink,
      Fill all my hunger, quench all my thirst;
      Flood me with joy, be the strength of my life,
      Fill all my hunger, quench all my thirst.

2   Thou art the food and the water of life,
    Thou canst revive me, my spirit upbear;
    I long to eat and to drink here of Thee,
    Thyself enjoy through my reading and prayer.

3   Thou art the Word with God's fulness in Thee,
    Thou too the Spirit that God my life be;
    Thee in the Word I enjoy as my food,
    Thou as the Spirit art water to me.

4   Thou from the heavens as food camest down,
    Thou to be drink hast been smitten for me;
    Thou as the food, my exhaustless supply,
    Thou as the water, a stream unto me.

5   Thou in the Word art the Spirit and life,
    Thus by the Word I may feed upon Thee;
    Thou dost as Spirit in my spirit live,
    Thus I may drink in the spirit of Thee.

6   Now to enjoy Thee I come to Thy Word,
    On Thee to feed till my hunger is o'er.
    Now in my spirit I turn unto Thee,
    Of Thee to drink till I'm thirsty no more.

7   Feeding and drinking, Lord Jesus, of Thee,
    Feeding by reading, and drinking by prayer;
    Reading and praying, I eat and I drink,
    Praying and reading—Lord, Thou art my fare.

8   Here, O my Lord, may I feast upon Thee;
    Flood with Thy Spirit and fill by Thy Word;
    May, Lord, Thou be such a feast unto me
    As man hath never enjoyed nor e'er heard.

*Composition for prophecy with main point and sub-points:* _____

_____

_____

_____

_____

_____

_____

_____

_____

_____

_____

_____

_____

_____

_____

_____

_____

_____

_____

_____

_____

_____

_____

_____

_____

_____

_____

_____

_____

_____

_____

_____

_____

_____

### The Preciousness of Zion and Jerusalem and the Situation of the Overcomers in Zion

Scripture Reading: Psa. 122:1; 125:1-2; 127:1; 128:5; 131:2; 132

Day 1    I. **Among the Old Testament types, there is God's holy city, Jerusalem, and within this city there is a high peak called Zion, on which the temple was built (Psa. 2:6; 125:1):**

A. Although God is mysterious and invisible, there are two earthly signs of God's existence—Zion and Jerusalem.

B. Psalms 120 through 134 indicate that Zion, the center, and Jerusalem, the circumference, remained deeply in the consideration of the people of Israel; they were very concerned for Zion and Jerusalem (137:1, 5-6).

C. On Mount Zion we have the church—the Body of Christ—and God's economy for God's testimony (Heb. 12:18-24).

II. **Jerusalem typifies the church, and Mount Zion typifies the overcomers in the church (Psa. 2:6; 20:2; 48:11-12; 53:6a; 87:2):**

A. Zion is the highlight of Jerusalem, the beauty of the holy city (48:2; 50:2).

B. The characteristics, the life, the blessing, and the establishment of Jerusalem come from Zion (51:18; 102:21; 128:5; 135:21; Isa. 41:27; Joel 3:17).

Day 2    C. In the New Testament the overcomers are likened to Zion; in Revelation 14:1 the one hundred forty-four thousand overcomers are not just in Jerusalem—they are on the peak of Zion.

D. In the church age the God-men who have been perfected and matured are Zion, the overcomers (v. 1):

1. The church is the heavenly Jerusalem, and the overcomers are Zion as the high peak and the highlight (Heb. 12:22; Rev. 14:1).

2. The church life is today's Jerusalem, and in the church there must be a group of overcomers; these overcomers are today's Zion.

3. The overcomers are for the building up of the Body of Christ to consummate the New Jerusalem (Rom. 12:4-5; Eph. 4:16; Rev. 3:12).

4. The overcomers conquer the satanic chaos in the old creation and carry out the divine economy for the new creation (1 Tim. 1:4; Eph. 1:10; 3:9-10; 2 Cor. 5:17; Gal. 6:15).

5. The Lord needs the overcomers to carry out the economy of God to have a Body and to destroy His enemy (Eph. 1:10; 3:9-10; Rev. 12:11).

*Day 3*

6. Without the overcomers the Body of Christ cannot be built up, and unless the Body of Christ is built up, Christ cannot come back for His bride (Eph. 4:16; 5:23, 27, 32; Rev. 19:7-9).

E. The Lord's recovery is to build up Zion (14:1; Eph. 4:16; Rev. 21:2):

1. Zion is the reality of the Body of Christ consummating in the New Jerusalem, and in the Lord's recovery today we must endeavor to reach this high peak (Eph. 1:22-23; 4:4-6, 16; Rev. 21:2).

2. The highest peak in God's economy is Zion, the reality of the Body of Christ, and in the church life we need to reach this high peak (Rom. 12:4-5; 1 Cor. 1:2; 12:12-13, 27).

3. The reality of the Body of Christ (Zion) is the corporate living of the perfected God-men, who are genuine men but live by the life of the processed and consummated Triune God, whose attributes are expressed through their virtues (Gal. 2:20; Phil. 3:10; 1:19-21a).

F. In the new heaven and new earth, the entire New Jerusalem will become Zion; the New Jerusalem, the eternal Mount Zion, will be the Holy of Holies, the place where God is (Rev. 21:1-2, 16, 22; cf. Ezek. 48:35).

G. The only way to reach the high peak of Zion is by praying; in order to reach Zion by praying, we need to know the significance of prayer for the carrying out of God's economy (1 Tim. 1:4; 2:8):

    1. Prayer is man breathing God, obtaining God, and being obtained by God; real prayer is an exhaling and inhaling before God, causing us and God to contact each other and to gain each other (1 Thes. 5:17).

    2. Prayer is man cooperating and co-working with God, allowing God to express Himself and His desire from within him and through him and thus accomplish His purpose (Rom. 8:26-27; James 5:17; Eph. 1:16-23; 3:14-21).

*Day 4*   III. **In the Psalms of Ascents—Psalms 120 through 134—we see the preciousness of Zion and Jerusalem to the saints; in all these psalms the house and the city are the center:**

    A. In Psalm 122 we see the saints' love for the house of God in Jerusalem (v. 1).

    B. Psalm 125 speaks concerning Jehovah's surrounding of His people:

      1. Those who trust in Jehovah are like Mount Zion, which cannot be moved but abides forever; they love Mount Zion and liken themselves to Mount Zion (v. 1).

      2. As the mountains surround Jerusalem, so Jehovah surrounds His people from now and to eternity (v. 2).

    C. Psalm 127 reveals Jehovah's care for and blessing to His people; instead of laboring in ourselves, we should trust in God, for He will take care of us and He will bless us.

*Day 5*     D. Psalm 128 speaks of Jehovah's blessing to Israel from Zion; God always blesses people from Zion, that is, from the overcomers (v. 5; cf. Num. 6:23-27).

    E. In Psalm 131 a saint speaks about his humbled heart and quieted soul before Jehovah:

      1. The psalmist has calmed and quieted his soul within him; he has been weaned, or stripped, of everything except the Lord (v. 2).

      2. When our heart is humbled and our soul is

quiet, we are in a condition that is suitable for God to come in to rest (132:14):

    a. In such a situation God can have a resting place, a dwelling (v. 14).

    b. Only when we are humble, calm, and quiet is the situation right for God to rise up, enter us, and take us as His resting place; this is Zion becoming God's habitation, His resting place, as revealed in Psalm 132.

*Day 6*   **IV. Psalm 132 speaks concerning Jehovah's habitation and rest in Zion through David (typifying Christ) His anointed:**

  A. In verses 2 through 5 we see David's desire for the house of God.

  B. David wanted Jehovah to arise and enter with the Ark into His resting place in Zion; today this resting place is the overcomers in the churches (vv. 6-8).

  C. Verses 7 and 8 are figurative of the recovery of the church life:

    1. The Ark was separated from the tabernacle; this signifies that Christ was with the church but that He has been separated from the church.

    2. Now is the time for us all to say, "Arise, O Jehovah, unto Your resting place, / You and the Ark of Your strength" (v. 8).

  D. Verses 14 through 18 are Jehovah's speaking concerning Zion; this is a picture of the top church life—the situation of the overcomers in Zion, the highest peak of God's mountain:

    1. Psalm 132 mentions seven items related to the overcomers: resting in God, dwelling with God (v. 14), food for satisfaction (v. 15), glorious clothing (v. 16), the horn of victory (v. 17), the enlightening lamp (v. 17), and the shining crown (v. 18).

    2. These items portray the situation of the overcomers in Zion, the highest peak of God's mountain.

## Morning Nourishment

**Psa.** But I have installed My King upon Zion, My holy
**2:6** mountain.
**125:1-2** Those who trust in Jehovah are like Mount Zion,
which cannot be moved *but* abides forever. Jerusalem—mountains surround her; and Jehovah surrounds His people from now and to eternity.

Among the Old Testament types there is God's holy city, Jerusalem, which is common and general. Within this city there is a
high peak called Zion (Psa. 2:6; 125:1). Zion is the highlight of
Jerusalem. Today the church is the heavenly Jerusalem (Heb.
12:22), and the overcomers are Zion as the high peak, the highlight. If all the believers are common and general, the church will
be merely Jerusalem without a high peak, without Zion. Such a
situation is not beautiful. Jerusalem's beauty is with Zion. Zion is
the beauty of the holy city (Psa. 48:2; 50:2). (*The Organic Union in
God's Relationship with Man*, p. 53)

## Today's Reading

Whereas Psalm 119 talks about the law, in [Psalms 120
through 134] the law is not mentioned. Instead...these psalms
refer to the matter of captivity. The people of Israel loved the law,
but they did not live according to the law. After they received the
law, their sins, offenses, and transgressions increased. They even
went so far as to turn from God and worship idols. For instance,
Judges 17 tells us of a man who set up idols in his home, who
appointed one of his sons to be his priest, and who later hired a
Levite to be a priest in his house. Since the people of Israel wanted
to worship idols, God caused them to go into captivity in a land of
idols. As the people were suffering in captivity, they forgot many
things, but they could not forget Zion and Jerusalem.

At that time, Mount Zion and Jerusalem, which was built on
Zion, were the only signs left on earth of God. Zion was the place
where Abraham offered his son Isaac; it was also the place chosen
by David. God is invisible, mysterious, and very deep. No one has
seen Him. Nevertheless, Zion and Jerusalem were earthly signs of

God's existence....Zion, the center, and Jerusalem, the circumference, remained deeply in the consideration of the people of Israel....Because of their experiences, the saints could not forget Zion and Jerusalem, and in their praises they did not neglect them. The saints were concerned not for godliness or comfort but for the fate of Zion and Jerusalem. (*Life-study of the Psalms,* pp. 465-466)

Jerusalem typifies the church. Within Jerusalem, there was Mount Zion. One typifies the whole body of the church, while the other typifies the overcomers of the church....Whenever there is something that has to do with God's heart desire, Zion is mentioned. Whenever there is something that has to do with the failures and sins of the Jews, Jerusalem is mentioned. God always allowed Jerusalem to be trodden down, but He always protected Zion. There is a New Jerusalem, but there never will be a new Zion, because Zion can never become old. Every time the Old Testament speaks of the relationship between Zion and Jerusalem, it shows us that the characteristics, the life, the blessing, and the establishment of Jerusalem come from Zion. In 1 Kings 8:1, the elders were in Jerusalem, and the Ark of the Covenant was in Zion. Psalm 51:18 says that God did good to Zion and built the walls of Jerusalem. Psalm 102:21 says that the name of the Lord was in Zion and that His praise was in Jerusalem. Psalm 128:5 says that the Lord blessed out of Zion and that the good was seen in Jerusalem. Psalm 135:21 says that the Lord dwelt at Jerusalem but that the Lord was to be blessed out of Zion. In Isaiah 41:27 the word was first announced to Zion and then preached to Jerusalem. Joel 3:17 says that when God dwelt in Zion, Jerusalem would be holy.

Today God is looking for the one hundred and forty-four thousand amidst the defeated church, who will stand on Mount Zion (Rev. 14). God always uses a small number of believers to pass on the flow of life to the church and to revive the church. (*The Collected Works of Watchman Nee,* vol. 11, pp. 762-763)

*Further Reading: The Collected Works of Watchman Nee, vol. 11, pp. 755-781*

## *Enlightenment and inspiration:* _____

_____
_____
_____

## Morning Nourishment

**Rev. And I saw, and behold, the Lamb standing on
14:1 Mount Zion, and with Him a hundred and forty-
four thousand, having His name and the name of
His Father written on their foreheads.**

**12:11 And they overcame him because of the blood of the
Lamb and because of the word of their testimony,
and they loved not their soul-life even unto death.**

The overcomers are the beauty of a local church. In each local church there must be a group of believers who ripen earlier to be the firstfruits. These believers are Zion in that church. Although it is wonderful to have the church in many localities, we like to see the beauty, the highlight, the high peak, the body of overcomers, in all the churches. Overcomers are what the Lord is after today. The Lord is after the overcomers to stand up, to ripen early. (*The Organic Union in God's Relationship with Man*, p. 53)

## Today's Reading

The good situation in the recovery today is just like Jerusalem. However, there is no Zion. In the New Testament the overcomers are likened to Zion. In Revelation 14:1 the 144,000 overcomers are not just in Jerusalem; they are on the peak of Zion. The overcomers, the vital groups, are today's Zion. My burden today is to help you reach the peak of the vital groups, that is, the overcomers' Zion. Although we may have a good church life, among us there is almost no realization, no practicality, no actuality, and no reality of the Body life. This is the need in the recovery today.

The many believers who were not perfected and matured in the church age will be perfected and matured in the kingdom age by God's disciplinary dealing....Not one believer can participate in the New Jerusalem without being perfected and matured. So in the thousand years of the kingdom age, God exercises His sovereignty to discipline these dear ones, to deal with them in many ways, in order that He could perfect them to make them mature. At the end of the thousand years, they will be ready to join the ones who were matured earlier in participating in the New Jerusalem. Today in the church age, the God-men who are perfected and matured are Zion, the overcomers, the vital groups within the churches. (*The Practical Points concerning Blending,* pp. 17, 45)

The stage of incarnation produced a group of redeemed people, and the stage of inclusion produced the church. The stage of intensification will build up the Body to consummate the New Jerusalem. [The overcomers are for this.] (*Incarnation, Inclusion, and Intensification,* p. 20)

In order to be the overcomers, we must conquer all the destructive chaos and triumph in the unique constructive economy....The overcomers are those who suffer the chaos, but they are not disappointed or discouraged. Instead, they are strengthened and enabled to stand for and live out the divine economy.

We have to conquer the satanic chaos by the processed and consummated Triune God as the all-sufficient grace....Paul said that the grace of the Lord was with him,...that the grace of the Lord Jesus Christ is with our spirit, and...that the Lord is with our spirit (1 Cor. 15:10; Gal. 6:18; 2 Tim. 4:22). The Lord as the all-sufficient grace is with our spirit, and we can conquer all the satanic chaos and carry out the unique divine economy by Him as our all-sufficient grace. (*The Satanic Chaos in the Old Creation and the Divine Economy for the New Creation,* pp. 75-76)

We need to be the overcomers, the ones who overcome all the negative things. The Lord has been delayed because He still needs some who will pay the price to be His overcomers. He told us clearly that He would come quickly. Of course, to Him one thousand years is like one day (2 Pet. 3:8). But still the Lord has not come back, because we have delayed Him. He needs the overcomers to carry out the economy of God to have a Body and to destroy His unique enemy. This is exactly why the book of Revelation was written. (*The Problems Causing the Turmoils in the Church Life,* pp. 27-28)

*Further Reading: The Satanic Chaos in the Old Creation and the Divine Economy for the New Creation,* chs. 1-2

## *Enlightenment and inspiration:* _____
_____
_____
_____

## Morning Nourishment

Rev. Let us rejoice and exult, and let us give the glory to
19:7 Him, for the marriage of the Lamb has come, and
His wife has made herself ready.
1 Tim. I desire therefore that men pray in every place, lift-
2:8 ing up holy hands, without wrath and reasoning.

[God's organic] salvation is for producing the overcomers to
build up the Body of Christ for the initial consummation of the
New Jerusalem in the kingdom age (Rev. 2:7) and the full consummation of the New Jerusalem in the new heaven and new
earth (21:2). As we look at the situation of today's Christians, we
may wonder who will build up the Body of Christ. Without the
overcomers the Body of Christ cannot be built up, and unless the
Body of Christ is built up, Christ cannot come back for His bride.
Christ will come back not only as the Savior but also as the
Bridegroom to marry His bride, who will be the totality of the
overcomers. (*The Secret of God's Organic Salvation, "The Spirit
Himself with Our Spirit,"* pp. 87-88)

## Today's Reading

We need to check whether or not we are doing everything in the
Spirit and having our being according to such a Spirit....The reality of the Body of Christ is the aggregate, the totality, of such a living by a group of God-men. This kind of a living, which is the reality
of the Body of Christ, will close this age, the age of the church, and
will bring Christ back to take, possess, and rule over this earth with
these God-men in the kingdom age. They were perfected, completed, and consummated in the church age. So in the next age, the
kingdom age, they will reign with Christ for a thousand years (Rev.
20:4-6)....We all have to endeavor to reach this high peak.

Such a life was there originally just in an individual man, Jesus
Christ. But this life has now been repeated, reproduced, in many
men who have been redeemed and regenerated and who now possess the divine life within them. All of them have been nourished,
sanctified, transformed, and perfected not just to be matured
Christians, but to be God-men. The reality of the Body of Christ is

the corporate living by the perfected God-men, who are genuine men but are not living by their life, but by the life of the processed God, whose attributes have been expressed through their virtues.

In the new heaven and new earth, there will be no more Zion, only Jerusalem, because all the unqualified saints will have been qualified to be Zion. In other words, the entire New Jerusalem will become Zion. What is Zion? Zion is the very spot where God is, that is, the Holy of Holies.

There is no other way to reach this high peak except by praying. It is more than evident that Jerusalem is here as a big realm of Christians, but where is Zion, the overcomers?...The overcomers are the very Zion, where God is. This is the intrinsic reality of the spiritual revelation in the holy Word of God. We have to realize what the Lord's recovery is. The Lord's recovery is to build up Zion. (*The Practical Points concerning Blending,* pp. 44-46, 35, 45-46)

Prayer is man breathing God, obtaining God, and being obtained by God. A real prayer is...man breathing in God just as he breathes in air. While you are thus breathing in God, spontaneously you are obtaining God, just as when you breathe in air you receive air. Consequently, not only is God obtained by you and becomes your enjoyment, but also your whole being surrenders to God, turns unto God, and is wholly gained by God. The more you pray, the more you will be filled with God, and the more you will surrender yourself to God and be gained by Him.

Real prayer...is an exhaling and inhaling before God, causing us and God, God and us, to contact one another and to obtain one another. Consequently, we wholly cooperate and work with God, and God expresses Himself and His desire through us, ultimately accomplishing His purpose. This is a fundamental meaning of prayer in the Bible.

Prayer is man cooperating and co-working with God, allowing God to express Himself and His desire through man, and thus accomplish His purpose. (*Lessons on Prayer,* pp. 15, 19, 17)

*Further Reading: The Practical Points concerning Blending,* chs. 4-5

## *Enlightenment and inspiration:* _____

_____

_____

_____

## *Morning Nourishment*

Psa. **Unless Jehovah builds the house, those who build**
127:1-2 **it labor in vain. Unless Jehovah keeps the city, the**
**guard watches in vain. It is vain for you to rise up**
**early, to stay up late, to eat the bread of toil; all the**
**same, He gives to His beloved while they sleep.**

Psalms 120—134 are a particular group known as the Songs
of Ascents. Instead of speaking concerning the law, these psalms
are related to the matter of captivity. The people of Israel loved
the law, but because they transgressed the law, even going so far
as to turn from God and worship idols (Jer. 2:13), God sent them
into captivity in a land of idols. As the people were suffering in
captivity, they could not forget Zion and Jerusalem, which were
signs, symbols, of the very God whom they worshipped. When
the people of Israel were captured, they were in a downward situation. To return to Jerusalem and to Zion was to be in an
upward situation, to "go up" (Psa. 122:4). Jerusalem was built on
Mount Zion. Therefore, when the people journeyed to Jerusalem, they had to ascend, and as they were ascending they sang a
song of ascents. (Psa. 120:1, footnote 1)

## *Today's Reading*

Psalm 122 is the praise of the saint in his going up to Zion
concerning his love of the house of God in Jerusalem. This is a
sweet psalm concerning the psalmist's love of the house of God.
This psalmist cared not for the law but for Zion and Jerusalem....The psalmist rejoiced when others said to him, "Let us go
to the house of Jehovah" (v. 1). Today we who love the church
should rejoice when someone says, "Let us go to the meeting."...In verses 2 through 4 we have the psalmist's praise of
Jerusalem, to which the tribes of Jehovah go up.

Psalm 125 is the praise of the saints in their going up to Zion
concerning Jehovah's surrounding of His people....In verse 1 the
psalmist says that those who trust in Jehovah are like Mount
Zion, which cannot be moved but abides forever. They loved
Mount Zion and they likened themselves to Mount Zion....

Verse 2 tells us that as the mountains surround Jerusalem, so Jehovah surrounds His people from now to eternity.

Psalm 127 is the praise of the saints in their going up to Zion concerning Jehovah's care for and blessing to His people. This Song of Ascents was written by Solomon.…In verses 1 and 2 we see Jehovah's care for His people.…"Unless Jehovah builds the house, / Those who build it labor in vain. / Unless Jehovah keeps the city, / The guard watches in vain" (v. 1). This is a comforting word, especially for the elders and for those who consider themselves guards protecting the church. Unless the Lord builds the church, those who build it labor in vain. Unless the Lord keeps the city—that is, keeps the church as the kingdom—those who guard the church watch in vain.…"It is vain for you to rise up early, / To stay up late, / To eat the bread of toil; / All the same, He gives to His beloved while they sleep" (v. 2). This indicates that if the Lord does not do anything for us, whatever we do will be in vain. Instead of toiling and striving in ourselves, we need to trust in Him, for He gives to His beloved even while they sleep. Do you believe that what you do means something? We need to realize that whatever we do without trusting in the Lord means nothing. If we realize this, we will rest in the Lord.

Psalm 127 is a psalm of release, a psalm that releases us from labor. This psalm teaches us that God takes care of us and blesses us. Whether we labor or do not labor, the situation is the same. "All the same," He gives to us while we sleep. In addition to caring for us, He blesses us with increase, with children. We all need to believe this. Even though I am a laboring person, I believe that the result depends not on my labor but on God's care and blessing.

Solomon's word in this psalm is directed at those who labor and endeavor to do things but do not trust in God. Instead of laboring in yourself, you should trust in God. He will take care of you, and He will bless you. (*Life-study of the Psalms*, pp. 469, 471-475)

*Further Reading: Life-study of the Psalms*, msg. 41; *The Vision of God's Building*, ch. 10

### *Enlightenment and inspiration:* _____
_____
_____
_____

## Morning Nourishment

Psa. **Jehovah bless you from Zion; and may you see the**
128:5 **prosperity of Jerusalem all the days of your life.**
131:1-2 **O Jehovah, my heart is not proud, nor are my eyes**
**haughty; nor do I go about in things too great or too**
**wondrous for me. Surely I have calmed and quieted**
**my soul, like a weaned child with its mother; like a**
**weaned child is my soul within me.**

The sequence of Psalms 128 through 134 is logical and rea-
sonable. We enjoy God's blessing from Zion and the prosperity of
Jerusalem, and then God deals with those who persecute us and
hate us. Nevertheless, we are sinful and need God's forgiveness.
When we receive His forgiveness, we become humble, calm, and
quiet, and God comes in to rest, to dwell, in us. Then we come up
to Him to dwell in unity. As a result, we become Mount Zion; that
is, we become the highest people, those who are even higher
than the priests.

Psalm 128 is the praise of a saint in his going up to Zion concerning Jehovah's blessing to Israel from Zion (signifying the
overcomers in the churches) and the prosperity of Jerusalem
(signifying the church as God's kingdom) in their enjoyment.
This indicates once again how precious are Zion and Jerusalem
in the experiences and praises of the saints. (*Life-study of the
Psalms*, pp. 478-479)

God always blesses His people from Zion, that is, from the
overcomers (cf. Num. 6:23-27…). (Psa. 128:5, footnote 2)

## Today's Reading

"Blessed is everyone who fears Jehovah, / Who walks in His
ways. / You will indeed eat the labor of your hands; / You will be
blessed, and it will go well with you" (Psa. 128:1-2)….Food and
peace are two basic elements for our daily life. If we lack food, we
will not have peace….According to verse 3, their wives will be like
fruitful vines in the innermost parts of their houses, and their
children will be like olive shoots round about their tables. In this
way will the man be blessed who fears Jehovah (v. 4)….Jehovah

will bless them from Zion, and they will see the prosperity of Jerusalem all the days of their life. They will also see the children of their children under the peace of God upon Israel (vv. 5-6).

Psalm 131 is the praise of the saint in his going up to Zion concerning his humbled heart and quieted soul before Jehovah....In verse 1 the psalmist says that his heart is not proud, nor are his eyes haughty. He also says that he does not go about in things too great or too wondrous for him. Certain things are too great and wondrous for us, and we should not go about in these things.... The psalmist continues by saying that he has calmed and quieted his soul within him...(v. 2). He had been weaned, or stripped, of everything except the Lord....The psalmist then advises Israel, God's chosen people, to hope in Jehovah from now to eternity (v. 3). When we have become like the psalmist, humble, calm, quiet, and weaned, we can advise others to hope in God.

The sequence of these seven psalms is significant. Psalm 128 speaks of Jehovah's blessing to Israel from Zion and the prosperity of Jerusalem in Israel's enjoyment....Psalm 131 indicates that after we experience God's forgiveness, we become humble. Formerly, we were proud and even haughty, thinking that we alone were right and that others were wrong. But after we are enlightened concerning our real situation, make a thorough confession, and receive God's forgiveness, we become humble....I have had this experience many times, realizing that I am nothing, that I have nothing, and that I can do nothing. When our heart is humbled and our soul is quiet, we are in a condition that is suitable for God to come in to rest....However, when we are proud and our eyes are haughty, God has no rest, no dwelling place, in us. Only when we are humble, calm, and quiet is the situation right for God to rise up, enter into us, and take us as His resting place. This is Zion becoming God's habitation, His resting place, as revealed in Psalm 132. (*Life-study of the Psalms,* pp. 479, 481-482, 477-478)

*Further Reading: Life-study of the Psalms,* msg. 42; *The Problems Causing Turmoils in the Lord's Recovery,* chs. 3-4

## *Enlightenment and inspiration:* _____

_____
_____
_____

## Morning Nourishment

**Psa.** **Arise, O Jehovah, unto Your resting place, You and**
**132:8-9** **the Ark of Your strength. Let Your priests be clothed**
**with righteousness, and let Your faithful ones give a**
**ringing shout.**

Psalm 132 is the praise of the saint in his going up to Zion
concerning Jehovah's habitation and rest in Zion through David
(typifying Christ) His anointed....In verse 1 the psalmist asks
Jehovah to remember all of David's afflictions, which typify all
the afflictions of Christ....Verses 2 through 5 show us David's
desire for the habitation of God (cf. 69:9a). David swore to Jehovah and vowed to the Mighty One of Jacob that he would not go
into the tent of his house, go up onto the couch of his bed, or give
sleep to his eyes or slumber to his eyelids until he found "a place
for Jehovah, / A tabernacle for the Mighty One of Jacob" (132:5).
Here "tabernacle" means a habitation....David sought for the
Ark, and he found it in Jaar. He then wanted Jehovah to arise
and enter with the Ark into His resting place in Zion (vv. 5-9, 13).
Today this resting place is the overcomers in the churches. (*Life-
study of the Psalms,* pp. 482-483)

## Today's Reading

In Psalm 129 we have the haters of Zion, but in Psalm 132
we see the lovers of God's dwelling place. David is the represen-
tative....The Ark had been removed from the tabernacle and
captured by the enemy, and even when the Ark was returned to
the children of Israel, it was not yet put into its proper place,
the tabernacle. A full recovery was needed. David was one who
loved God so deeply, one who was devoted to God's resting
place, to God's habitation. He said that he would not enter his
house until the Lord could find a habitation; he would not take
sleep until the Lord should find rest.

Verses 7 and 8 say, "We will go into His tabernacle; / We will
worship at His footstool. / Arise, O Jehovah, unto Your resting
place, / You and the Ark of Your strength." This is figurative of
the recovery of the church life. The Ark was separated from the

tabernacle, which signifies Christ separated from the church life....This is the time when we must all say, "Lord, arise; return unto Your resting place, the local churches."

Verse 13 says, "Jehovah has chosen Zion; / He has desired it for His habitation." Zion, which represents the local churches, is the choice of God, the desire of God. This word in verse 13 is the word of the psalmist, but when we continue into verse 14, we see that it is also the word of the Lord Himself. (*Christ and the Church Revealed and Typified in the Psalms,* pp. 206-207)

Verses 14 through 18 are Jehovah's speaking concerning Zion. "This is My resting place forever; / Here will I dwell, for I have desired it" (v. 14). I hope that one day God will say such a word to you. Jehovah continues by saying that He will abundantly bless Zion's provision and satisfy its poor with bread, that He will clothe its priests with salvation, that its saints will shout with a ringing shout, that there He will cause the horn of David to shoot forth, that He has prepared a lamp for His Anointed One, and that He will clothe with shame the enemies of His Anointed One but that on Him His crown will shine.

In this psalm we have seven items related to the over-comer—resting, dwelling, food, clothing, the victorious horn, the enlightening lamp, and the shining crown. These items are at the top of the church life. When we are at the top of the church life, we have the resting with God, the dwelling, and the food. However, when God is homeless, we also are homeless. When He does not have satisfaction, we also do not have satisfaction. But when God is resting and dwelling in Zion, we have plenty of food. Furthermore, we have the proper clothing, a horn, a lamp, and a crown. This is the top church life. This is the situation of the overcomers in Zion, the highest peak of God's mountain. (*Life-study of the Psalms,* p. 483)

Further Reading: Christ and the Church Revealed and Typified in the Psalms, ch. 21; The Satanic Chaos in the Old Creation and the Divine Economy in the New Creation, chs. 3-4

*Enlightenment and inspiration:* _____
_____
_____
_____

### *Hymns,* #1248

1   Recall how David swore,
    "I'll not come into my house,
    Nor go up to my bed,
    Give slumber to mine eyelids,
    Until I find a place for Thee,
    A place, O Lord, for Thee."
    Our mighty God desires a home
    Where all His own may come.

2   How blinded we have been,
    Shut in with what concerns us;
    While God's house lieth waste—
    Lord, break through, overturn us;
    We'll go up to the mountain,
    Bring wood and build the house;
    We'll never say, "Another day!"
    It's time! We'll come and build!

3   O Lord, against these days,
    Inspire some for Your building,
    Just as in David's day—
    A remnant who are willing
    To come and work in Your house,
    Oh, what a blessed charge!
    Your heart's desire, is our desire—
    We come, O Lord, to build.

4   Within those whom You'd call
    Put such a restless caring
    For building to give all—
    These times are for preparing;
    *The gates of hell cannot prevail*
    *Against the builded Church!*
    The hours are few, the builders too—
    Lord, build, O build in us!

*Composition for prophecy with main point and sub-points:* _____

## Jehovah's Commanded Blessing of Life
## on Brothers Who Dwell Together in Oneness

Scripture Reading: Psa. 133—134

*Day 1*   I. **Psalm 133 is the praise of a saint, in his going up to Zion, concerning Jehovah's commanded blessing of life on brothers who dwell together in oneness; the blessing that is commanded whenever brothers are united under the anointing is "life forever," a full, free, unceasing stream of life:**

A. The brothers' dwelling together in oneness is likened to the inestimable goodness of the precious ointment on the head of Aaron and to the incalculable pleasantness of the dew of Hermon on the mountains of Zion (vv. 1-3):

1. As a person typified by Aaron, the church as the one new man includes the Head with the Body as the corporate Christ, the corporate priesthood (Eph. 2:15; 1 Pet. 2:5).

2. As a place typified by Zion, the church is the dwelling place of God (Deut. 12:5-7, 11, 14, 18, 21, 26; Eph. 2:21-22; Rev. 21:3, 22).

B. The genuine all-inclusive oneness (the oneness of the all-inclusive Spirit) is constituted with the spreading ointment and the descending dew for the gradual building up of Christ's Body in the divine dispensing of the Divine Trinity:

*Day 2*    1. Psalm 133 is equivalent to Ephesians 4; when we are in the Body and are diligent to keep the oneness of the Spirit, we have the anointing of the all-inclusive Spirit (vv. 3-6); the anointing oil as the compound ointment is a type of the processed Triune God, the all-inclusive compound Spirit (Exo. 30:23-25):

a. The compound Spirit is the ultimate consummation of the processed Triune God with the divine attributes, the human virtues, Christ's death with its effectiveness, and Christ's resurrection with its power (Phil. 1:19).

b. We are in the oneness that is the processed Triune God anointed, or "painted," into our being (2 Cor. 1:21-22; 1 John 2:20, 27).

c. Day by day in the church life, all the ingredients of the divine and mystical compound ointment are being wrought into us; through the application of these ingredients to our inward being, we are spontaneously in the all-inclusive oneness (Eph. 4:3-4).

*Day 3*
*&*
*Day 4*

d. The ground of oneness is simply the processed Triune God applied to our being; the anointing of the compound, all-inclusive life-giving Spirit is the element of our oneness (v. 4; cf. John 4:24):

1) If we act apart from the Spirit, who is in our spirit, we are divisive and lose the oneness (Eph. 4:3; cf. 1 Cor. 1:10; 2:14-15; 3:1).

2) If we stay in the life-giving Spirit, we keep the oneness of the Spirit (cf. John 4:24; 1 Cor. 6:17).

e. The compound Spirit is not for those who are individualistic; He is in and for the Body and for the priestly service that builds up the Body (Psa. 133:2; Exo. 30:26-31; Phil. 1:19; Rom. 15:16; 1 Pet. 2:5, 9).

2. The dew of Hermon descending on the mountains of Zion signifies the descending, refreshing, watering, and saturating grace of life (3:7), the Triune God as our life supply for our enjoyment (2 Cor. 13:14):

a. In typology Hermon signifies the heavens, the highest place in the universe (cf. Eph. 1:3; Matt. 17:1-2).

*Day 5*

b. The mountains of Zion typify the local churches; there is one Zion, one church as one Body, but many mountains, many local churches (Rev. 1:11-12).

  c. Grace is God in Christ as the Spirit experienced, received, enjoyed, and gained by us (John 1:16-17; 1 Cor. 15:10; Gal. 2:20-21; Rom. 5:2, 17, 21).

  d. By remaining in the church life, we are preserved in the Lord's grace (Acts 4:33; 11:23).

  e. By the grace we receive on the mountains of Zion, we can live a life that is impossible for people in the world to live (20:32; 2 Cor. 12:7-9).

  f. The Christian living must be the living of grace, the experience of grace (1:12; 1 Cor. 15:10; 2 Tim. 4:22):

    1) We have faith and love through the Lord's superabounding grace (1 Tim. 1:14).

    2) By grace we receive the salvation in life through Christ's resurrection and ascension (Eph. 2:5-8).

    3) We have obtained access into and stand in God's abounding grace (Rom. 5:2).

    4) In this grace we can enjoy God's eternal comfort and good hope (2 Thes. 2:16).

    5) We can come forward with boldness to the throne of grace to find grace for timely help (Heb. 4:16; cf. Eph. 2:22).

    6) We can receive God's abounding supply of all grace (2 Cor. 9:8).

    7) We can constantly enjoy God's multiplying grace (1 Pet. 1:2b; 2 Pet. 1:2; Rev. 22:21).

    8) We can enjoy God's greater grace through humility (James 4:6; 1 Pet. 5:5).

    9) In our experience of the grace in God's economy, we enjoy the Lord's presence in our spirit (2 Tim. 4:22; cf. Luke 1:28, 30).

    10) We need to live out Christ as God's righteousness by the grace of God (Gal. 2:20-21).

    11) We need to experience the perfecting of the Lord's sufficient grace, Christ's overshadowing power, in our weakness (2 Cor. 12:9).

    12) By grace we can overcome the usurpation of temporal and uncertain riches and become generous in ministering to the needy saints (8:1-2).

    13) The God of all grace perfects, establishes, strengthens, and grounds us through our sufferings (1 Pet. 5:10).

    14) We need to be good stewards of the varied grace of God (4:10; Eph. 3:2).

    15) Our word should convey Christ as grace to others (4:29-30).

    16) We need to experience Christ as grace to be a surpassing one and to labor abundantly for the Lord (1 Cor. 15:10).

    17) We need to receive the abundance of grace and of the gift of righteousness to reign in life (Rom. 5:17, 21).

  g. The grace given to the local churches in the dark age of the church's degradation is for the believers who seek to answer the Lord's calling to be His overcomers (Rev. 1:4).

  h. The grace of the Lord Jesus Christ dispensed to His believers throughout the New Testament age consummates in the New Jerusalem as the consummation of God's good pleasure in joining and mingling Himself with man for His enlargement and eternal expression (22:21).

3. In the church life we are daily anointed and graced (Eph. 1:13, 6).

4. The anointing of the Spirit and the supply of grace make it possible for us to live in oneness.

5. The more we experience Christ as the life-giving Spirit, the more our natural constitution and disposition are reduced; as they are reduced through our experience of the Triune God with His divine attributes, we are perfected into one (John 17:23; Eph. 4:1-3).

*Day 6* II. **As the conclusion to Psalm 133 and as the last of the Songs of Ascents, Psalm 134 is the praise of a saint, in his going up to Zion, concerning the charge and the blessing of the children of Israel to the serving priests in the house of God:**

A. Psalm 134 indicates that the highest people, those who are in Zion, can bless everyone and teach everyone (vv. 1-2; cf. Gen. 47:10; 48:20; 49:28).

B. The blessing comes from Zion, from the highest peak, from the ones who have attained to the top, to the position of the overcomers (Psa. 134:3).

C. In every age and century God's blessing has come to the church because of the overcomers (cf. Rev. 2:7; Num. 6:23-27).

## Morning Nourishment

**Psa.** **For Jehovah has chosen Zion; He has desired it for**
**132:13-16** **His habitation. This is My resting place forever; here**
**will I dwell, for I have desired it. I will abundantly**
**bless its provision; I will satisfy its poor with bread.**
**And its priests I will clothe with salvation, and its**
**faithful ones will shout with a ringing shout.**
**133:1** **Behold, how good and how pleasant it is for broth-**
**ers to dwell in unity!**

Psalm 133 is the praise of a saint, in his going up to Zion, concerning Jehovah's commanded blessing on brothers who dwell in
oneness. When Zion is built up and when God is resting there and
dwelling in Jerusalem, as depicted in Psalm 132, we have a place
where we can gather and where we can dwell together in oneness.
How good and how pleasant this is!

In this psalm the believers' dwelling together in oneness is likened to the inestimable goodness of the precious ointment on the
head of Aaron and to the incalculable pleasantness of the dew of
Hermon on the mountains of Zion.

The unity spoken of here is a picture of the genuine oneness in
the New Testament. This oneness is the processed and consummated Triune God mingled with the believers in Christ (John
17:21-23). Since the Body of Christ is such a mingling (Eph. 4:4-6),
the Body itself is the oneness. According to the picture in this
psalm, the genuine oneness is constituted of the spreading ointment and the descending dew for the gradual building up of the
Body of Christ in the divine dispensing of the Divine Trinity. (Psa.
133:1, footnotes 1-3)

## Today's Reading

[In Psalm 133:1] the psalmist uses two adjectives to describe
brethren dwelling together in oneness....These two adjectives
point to two aspects of oneness. The oneness is good and pleasant:
good as the precious ointment and pleasant as the descending dew.

Of these aspects, the first—Aaron—is a person, and the second—Zion—is a place....The church has these two aspects. On the

one hand, the church is a person; on the other hand, the church is a place. As a person, the church includes the Head with the Body. As a place, the church is the dwelling place of God. Elsewhere in the Bible we see that the church is the bride, the new man, and the warrior. These, however, are aspects of the church as a person.

Verse 2...refers to the anointing oil described in Exodus 30. That anointing oil is a compound ointment formed by blending four spices with olive oil. Aaron, his sons, the tabernacle, and everything related to the tabernacle were anointed with this ointment. According to Psalm 133, this ointment, this compound anointing oil, was upon a person, Aaron....By contrast, the refreshing, watering, and saturating dew was on a place, the mountains of Zion.

Neither the anointing oil nor the saturating dew moved quickly. The dew did not fall down like rain; it descended, came down, in a gradual way. In like manner, the ointment did not actually run down upon Aaron's beard; it spread upon his beard and then went down to the skirts of his garments....Gently and slowly, the ointment spread. In the same principle the dew came down upon the mountains of Zion....The genuine oneness is constituted of the spreading ointment and the descending dew.

This picture of oneness is related to a person, Aaron, a type of Christ in His priestly ministry. As the High Priest, Christ served God, accomplished God's purpose, and fulfilled the desire of God's heart. However, in Psalm 133 Aaron typifies not only Christ Himself, but Christ with His Body. This means that here Aaron typifies the corporate Christ, the Head with the Body. The church in a very real sense is the corporate Christ. The church is thus a universal, great person with a number of aspects: the aspects of the Body, the Bride, the new man, and the warrior. All these aspects of the church are related to the person. (*The Genuine Ground of Oneness*, pp. 78-79, 87-88)

*Further Reading: The Genuine Ground of Oneness, ch. 6; Life-study of the Psalms, msg. 42*

### *Enlightenment and inspiration:* _____

_____
_____
_____

## *Morning Nourishment*

Eph. **Being diligent to keep the oneness of the Spirit in**
4:3-6 **the uniting bond of peace: one Body and one Spirit,**
**even as also you were called in one hope of your**
**calling; one Lord, one faith, one baptism; one God**
**and Father of all, who is over all and through all**
**and in all.**

In Ephesians 4:4-6 Paul lists seven aspects of oneness: one Body, one Spirit, one hope, one Lord, one faith, one baptism, and one God and Father. These verses also show the mysterious mingling of the Triune God with the Body of Christ. This mingling is the oneness of the believers. The Spirit in verse 4 is no doubt the compound, all-inclusive Spirit who is within the Body and gives life to the Body. According to 1 Corinthians 12:13, the Body came into existence through the baptism of this all-inclusive Spirit. Having been baptized in one Spirit, we must go on to drink of this Spirit. This indicates that the existence of the Body depends on the all-inclusive life-giving Spirit. Furthermore, the Body continues to exist through our drinking of this Spirit. Anything we drink becomes mingled with our inward being, with our blood and with the very fiber of our organic tissue. It is the same with the life-giving Spirit. (*The Genuine Ground of Oneness*, pp. 85-86)

## *Today's Reading*

The oneness...is the precious ointment upon Christ the Head and the refreshing dew that descends upon the mountains of Zion. It makes a tremendous difference whether we remain in this oneness or forsake it. Christians today feel free to come and go because they do not see this genuine oneness. They do not have the preserving and keeping element the oneness affords. In His recovery the Lord has shown us that real oneness is the mingling of the processed Triune God with His chosen people. On the one hand, the processed God is the compound, all-inclusive Spirit that anoints us and "paints" us day by day. On the other hand, the processed God is the life supply for our enjoyment. Under this anointing oil and watering dew we experience true oneness....Actually, this oneness [in Ephesians 4:3] is simply the all-inclusive, life-giving Spirit Himself. We guard and preserve this oneness by remaining under the anointing oil and the watering dew. (*The Genuine Ground of Oneness,* p. 96)

Psalm 133 is the key passage in the Old Testament concerning the anointing. We should realize that Psalms 120 through 134... are the songs the Israelites sang three times a year when they ascended from different places to meet the Lord in Zion in Jerusalem, the dwelling place of God....The people did not talk about economics, education, warfare, or politics. Their hearts were toward Zion, toward God, and they were going upward. Psalm 133:1 says, "Behold, how good and how pleasant it is / For brothers to dwell in unity!" This dwelling in unity is corporate; there is no barrier or separation. They have cast aside their disunity, jealousy, and hatred. This is like the fine oil that was poured on Aaron's head that ran down upon the beard to the hem of his garments. In this condition, they receive God's anointing. When the oil flows down, those who are under the head will spontaneously receive the oil. Psalm 133 is equivalent to Ephesians 4. When we are in the Body and are diligent to keep the oneness of the Spirit, we have the anointing of the Spirit. We have to come under the Head, and we have to live in the Body before we can receive the anointing. Many people do not receive any leading because they are not standing in the right place. They are not under the Head and have not submitted themselves to the authority of the Head. Neither are they in the Body. In order for us to receive the anointing, we must submit to the Head and live in the Body.

The believers' fellowship is based on Christ. We can fellowship with one another because Christ is the life of the Body and the Head of the Body. At the same time, the enjoyment of this fellowship is the Holy Spirit. The more we live in the fellowship of the Body, the more we enjoy the anointing of the Spirit. (*The Mystery of Christ,* pp. 41-42)

*Further Reading: The Mystery of Christ, chs. 7, 10*

*Enlightenment and inspiration:* _____

_____

_____

## Morning Nourishment

**Exo.** You also take the finest spices: of flowing myrrh...
**30:23-25** and of fragrant cinnamon...and of fragrant calamus...and of cassia...and a hin of olive oil. And you
shall make it a holy anointing oil, a fragrant ointment compounded...

**Phil.** For I know that for me this will turn out to salvation
**1:19** through your petition and *the* bountiful supply of
the Spirit of Jesus Christ.

Real oneness is the mingling of the processed God with the
believers. Although this is revealed in the New Testament, we
do not see in the New Testament the way to practice this oneness.
The way to practice this mingling is in Psalm 133. The ointment
in verse 2 is a type of the processed Triune God who today is the
all-inclusive compound Spirit. According to Exodus 30, the anointing oil is a compound formed by blending four spices with a hin of
olive oil. This compound typifies the all-inclusive Spirit who is the
processed God for our enjoyment. In this compound Spirit we
have not only divinity, but also Christ's humanity, the effectiveness of His death, and the power of His resurrection. In other
words, the compound Spirit is the processed God with the divine
attributes, the human virtues, the effectiveness of Christ's death,
and the power of Christ's resurrection. In the church life this compound Spirit is continually anointing us. (*The Genuine Ground of
Oneness*, pp. 79-80)

## Today's Reading

The ointment can be compared to paint, and the anointing to
the application of the paint....As the compound Spirit anoints us,
He "paints" us and the "paint" is the very Triune God. In this
"paint" we have the humanity of Christ, the effectiveness of
Christ's death, and the power of Christ's resurrection. We also
have Christ's divinity and human living. As all these ingredients
of the ointment are applied to us, we are "painted" with the
processed Triune God and with all the elements in the compound
ointment. The proper church life is a life in the oneness which is

the mingling of the processed Triune God with the believers. As we remain in this oneness, we are "painted" with the ointment. The more we are "painted" in this way, the more our natural constitution, temperament, and disposition are eliminated. What remains is the mingling of the processed Triune God with our uplifted humanity. This is the oneness.

In such a oneness it is not possible to have division, not even dissension. In this oneness there is no room even for our opinion. Although we need much more experience of the divine "painting" which brings us into oneness, we have had at least some experience of this in the church life. To a certain degree at least, we have all entered into the oneness.

When we were in the denominations or independent groups, we found it easy to be opinionated or critical. But in the church the dissenting element and divisive factors are subdued. This is the effect of oneness....Through the application of the heavenly "paint," we are brought into the genuine oneness, not the superficial oneness that is according to the natural concept. We are in the oneness which is the processed Triune God "painted" into our very being.

The anointing does not cause us to have very much feeling in our emotion. Those experiences that come and go quickly, on the contrary, stir up our feeling. But this is not the normal experience in the church life. In the church life we experience the gradual spreading of the all-inclusive ointment. For example, in the church prayer meeting we may receive one or two "coats" of "paint" without having much feeling of it....Day by day in the church life, all the ingredients of the divine ointment are being wrought into us. Through the application of these ingredients to our inward being, we are spontaneously in the oneness. We find it exceedingly difficult to be divisive or even dissenting. How good, lovely, and enjoyable is the oneness in the church!...We are one spontaneously because we have been "painted" with all the elements of the heavenly "paint." (*The Genuine Ground of Oneness,* pp. 80-81)

*Further Reading: Life-study of Philippians,* msg. 33

## *Enlightenment and inspiration:* _____

_____

_____

_____

## *Morning Nourishment*

Psa. 133:1-3  **Behold, how good and how pleasant it is for brothers to dwell in unity! It is like the fine oil upon the head that ran down upon the beard, upon Aaron's beard, that ran down upon the hem of his garments; like the dew of Hermon that came down upon the mountains of Zion. For there Jehovah commanded the blessing: life forever.**

The ground of oneness is simply the processed Triune God applied to our being. This is the oneness in which we find ourselves today. We are not in a oneness produced by adding together those who believe in Christ....Once we have been brought into the oneness produced by the application of the processed Triune God to our being, it is very difficult to have any subtraction....The oneness in Christianity involves addition and subtraction. But the oneness in the churches in the Lord's recovery involves the application of the Triune God to our inward being.

This oneness is made real and practical by means of the anointing that is upon Christ the Head and that spreads upon the Body. As long as we remain in the Body, we share the ointment. In this ointment we are one. Hence, the anointing of the compound, all-inclusive, life-giving Spirit is the element of our oneness. This means that to be one as members of the church is to be under the Spirit's anointing. If we are not under this anointing, we cannot be one with anyone, not even with ourselves. (*The Genuine Ground of Oneness*, pp. 81-82, 89-90)

## *Today's Reading*

The ointment is not for individuals; it is for the Body. It cannot be experienced by those who are separate and detached from the Body. According to the picture in Psalm 133, the ointment is upon the head. Then it spreads to the beard and goes down to the skirts of the garment. This indicates that if we are individualistic, we cannot experience the ointment. Some may argue that they can contact the Lord alone at home. No doubt they can. The crucial matter, however, is whether or not we are one with the church.

If we are one with the church, then we can properly contact the Lord alone at home. But if we separate ourselves from the church, our contact with the Lord will be altogether different. The reason is that the anointing oil is not for individualistic members; it is for the Head and the Body, even for the Head with the Body. Hence, to be "painted" by the ointment, we must be in the church. Then we spontaneously enjoy the application of the anointing oil with all its elements. How marvelous is the oneness produced by the application of this ointment!

According to Psalm 133:3, the oneness is also like the dew that descends upon the mountains of Zion. The anointing oil is upon the person, Aaron, but the dew is upon the place, Zion. The dew signifies the grace of life (1 Pet. 3:7)...[which] is the supply of life. In the church life we are not only under the anointing; we also receive the supply, the grace, of life. As we are anointed, we are also graced.

The apostle Paul abundantly experienced the Lord's grace. Three times he prayed that the "thorn" which was afflicting him would be removed. The Lord replied that His grace was sufficient for Paul. By this word the Lord indicated that He would not take away the thorn, but He would supply Paul with His sufficient grace [2 Cor. 12:7-10].

Second Corinthians 13:14...indicates that grace is the Triune God processed to be our life supply. Whereas the ointment signifies the processed Triune God who is "painted" into our being, the dew signifies the Triune God who is our life supply for our enjoyment. Therefore, in the church life daily we are anointed and graced. We are "painted" with the processed God, and we are graced with the very same processed God as our life supply. This anointing and this supply make it possible for us to live in oneness. In the words of Psalm 133, this oneness is like the anointing oil and the watering dew. Under the anointing oil and the watering dew, we experience the blessing of life on the ground of oneness. (*The Genuine Ground of Oneness*, pp. 82-83)

*Further Reading: The Genuine Ground of Oneness*, ch. 7

***Enlightenment and inspiration:*** _____

_____

_____

_____

## Morning Nourishment

Acts   And with great power the apostles gave testimony
4:33   of the resurrection of the Lord Jesus, and great
       grace was upon them all.

1 Tim.   And the grace of our Lord superabounded with
1:14     faith and love in Christ Jesus.

Rom.   ...Those who receive the abundance of grace and of
5:17   the gift of righteousness will reign in life through
       the One, Jesus Christ.

In Psalm 133 the oneness of God's people is also likened to
the dew of Hermon that descends upon the mountains of Zion.
These mountains typify the local churches. Every local church is
a mountain of Zion. There is one Zion, but many mountains signifying the many local churches. As a person, the church is
uniquely one. As a place, the church, on the one hand, is the
unique Zion; but, on the other hand, it is the many mountains of
the one Zion. Although there is one church in the universe, there
are nevertheless many local churches. Each local church is a
peak among the many mountains of Zion. Therefore, the person
is universal, but the mountains are local. Our oneness is like the
precious ointment upon Aaron and like the dew upon the mountains of Zion. God's dwelling place, the temple, was located in
Zion. On the one hand, the church is a person; on the other hand,
it is a place. Upon the person there is the ointment, and upon the
place there is the dew. (*The Genuine Ground of Oneness,* p. 88)

## Today's Reading

In the local churches we are daily under the dew, under the
grace....If we wish to enjoy this grace in full, we need to be in the
church life. According to Psalm 133, the grace does not descend
upon the homes of individual believers; it descends upon the
mountains of Zion, which typify the local churches. Thus, if we
would enjoy the dew that descends from Mount Hermon, we
need to be on one of the peaks of Zion....In the church life the
dew descends upon us richly. We are happy because we have the

abundant supply of the all-sufficient grace....By this grace we can live a life that it is impossible for people in the world to live. The brothers can love their wives to the uttermost, and the sisters can submit to their husbands in a full way. Such a living is possible through the grace we receive on the mountains of Zion. (*The Genuine Ground of Oneness,* pp. 94-95)

Grace is Christ. All the spiritual experiences of a Christian should be experiences of Christ as grace. In our experience of the grace in God's economy, first, we have faith and love through the Lord's superabounding grace (1 Tim. 1:14). To be a believer is a matter of faith and love. Faith and love are products of the Lord's grace. Through faith we receive the Lord, and through love we enjoy the Lord whom we have received. We have neither faith nor love, but when we allow the Lord to come into us, both faith and love from the Lord as grace come into us.

In their experience of the grace in God's economy, the believers also receive the salvation in life in Christ's resurrection and ascension (Eph. 2:5-8). This salvation is a salvation in life....This salvation is the resurrected and ascended Christ becoming our grace.

The believers' experience of the grace in God's economy enables them to obtain access into and stand in God's grace (Rom. 5:2a). Today we are not under the law but under the grace in God's economy. This grace is God Himself.

We reign in life by receiving the abundance of grace and of the gift of righteousness. This is grace reigning in life unto eternal life (Rom. 5:17b, 21b). The life we have received does not merely save us from a few things; rather, it enthrones us as kings to reign over all things. We have received righteousness objectively, but we still need to continually receive the abundance of grace so that we can reign in life subjectively....This is to overcome. This is grace reigning unto eternal life. (*The Law and Grace of God in His Economy,* pp. 35-37, 41)

*Further Reading: The Law and Grace of God in His Economy,* chs. 2-4; *The Genuine Ground of Oneness,* ch. 9

*Enlightenment and inspiration:* _____

_____

_____

_____

## Morning Nourishment

| | |
|---|---|
| Psa. 134:1-3 | **Bless Jehovah now, all you servants of Jehovah who stand by night in the house of Jehovah. Lift up your hands in the sanctuary, and bless Jehovah. May Jehovah, who made heaven and earth, bless you from Zion.** |

As the last of the Songs of Ascents, Psalm 134 is the praise of the saint in His going up to Zion concerning the charge and the blessing of the children of Israel to the serving priests in the house of God. This psalm indicates that the highest people, those who are in Zion, can bless everyone and teach everyone.

[Verses 1 and 2] are the charge of the children of Israel to the serving priests. Although these priests are serving in the house of God, they are lower than the ones in Zion. Thus, those in Zion can give such a charge to these servants of Jehovah.

"May Jehovah, who made heaven and earth, / Bless you from Zion" (v. 3). Here we see that the blessing comes from Zion, that is, from the highest people. If you read the history of the church, you will see that in every age and century God's blessing has come to the church because of the overcomers. Whenever there are some overcomers, there will be God's blessing. God always blesses His people from Zion, from the highest peak, from the ones who have attained to the top, to the position of the overcomers. From this position God blesses all His people. (*Life-study of the Psalms,* p. 485)

## Today's Reading

Both Psalm 133 and 134 have only three verses. They are short psalms, but how precious! Never before have I appreciated Psalm 134 as much as I do today. Psalm 133 is a continuation of Psalm 132, and Psalm 134 is the conclusion of Psalm 133. By the close of Psalm 132 God enters into His rest, and we obtain satisfaction in the habitation of God. Hence, following that, we have the church life in Psalm 133. Psalm 134 now is a conclusion to that wonderful church life presented in Psalm 133. "Bless

Jehovah now, / All you servants of Jehovah / Who stand by night in the house of Jehovah. / Lift up your hands in the sanctuary, / And bless Jehovah" (134:1-2). This was the word of the people to the priests. All the people were telling the priests, "All you servants of Jehovah, you must bless Jehovah." Then the last verse of Psalm 134 is the answer, the reply, of the priests to the people: "May Jehovah, who made heaven and earth, / Bless you from Zion." God's servants bless Him in His house, and God blesses His people from Zion. This little psalm means that we all must fellowship and communicate in this way. After a good meeting, after a rich enjoyment of Christ, some of us may say, "Bless the name of the Lord." Then others may answer, "The Lord bless you from Zion." How blessed! Let us try it. This is a good fellowship, a good communication, a good conclusion, to a meeting of the church. (*Christ and the Church Revealed and Typified in the Psalms,* pp. 209-210)

After Jacob became mature, he blessed whomever he met. Wherever he went, he did nothing except bless others. When Jacob was brought before Pharaoh, the first thing he did was bless him (Gen. 47:7). After talking a while with Pharaoh, Jacob blessed him again (v. 10). Jacob was not only a blessed person; he was also a blessing person. While it is easy to receive a blessing, it is not easy to bless others. A grandson cannot bless his grandfather, because the grandson lacks the maturity in life. Because Jacob was mature, he blessed everyone he met, including Pharaoh, who was an unbeliever, a Gentile king....His burden was simply to bless others.

The sign of the maturity of life is blessing....Complaining is a sign of immaturity. When you have matured, you will not complain; you will bless, saying, "O God, bless all the brothers and all the churches." For the one who is matured in life, the supplanting hand has become the blessing hand. The more mature you are, the more you will bless others. (*Life-study of Genesis,* pp. 819, 822)

*Further Reading: Christ and the Church Revealed and Typified in the Psalms,* ch. 21

### *Enlightenment and inspiration:* _____

_____

_____

_____

## *Hymns,* #1339

1  Behold how good and how pleasant it is,
   For brethren to dwell together in unity!
   Behold how good and how pleasant it is,
   For brethren to dwell together in unity!

   It is like the precious ointment upon the head,
   That ran down upon the beard,
   Even Aaron's beard:
   That went down to the skirts of his garments.

2  Behold how good and how pleasant it is,
   For brethren to dwell together in unity!

   It is like the precious ointment upon the head,
   That ran down upon the beard,
   Even Aaron's beard:
   That went down to the skirts of his garments.

3  As the dew of Hermon,
   And as the dew that descended
   Upon the mountains of Zion:
   For there the Lord commanded the blessing,
   Even life for evermore.

*Composition for prophecy with main point and sub-points:* _____

*The Recovery of the Earth
through God's Reigning
in Christ and His Kingdom*

Scripture Reading: Psa. 2:8-9; 8:1; 22:27-28; 48:1-2; 72:8,
19; 93:1; 97:1; 145:1, 11-13

*Day 1*  **I. It is crucial that we have a clear understanding of the extract, the spirit, of the Psalms (2:6-8; 26:8; 36:8-9; 46:4; 48:1-2; 72:8, 19):**

A. The spirit, the reality, the characteristic, of the divine revelation in the book of Psalms is Christ as the centrality and universality of the eternal economy of God (Luke 24:44).

B. Christ is first the embodiment of the Triune God, then the house, the habitation of God (signified by the temple), the kingdom of God (signified by the city of Jerusalem), and the Ruler of the entire earth from the house of God and in the kingdom of God (Psa. 2:6-8; 36:8-9; 46:4; 48:1-2; 72:8, 19).

C. God desires to have an organic habitation on earth, and this habitation is the aggregate of the saints gained by God through the terminating death and germinating resurrection of the all-inclusive Christ (22:22; 26:8):

1. The saints will be the eternal manifestation and expression of the processed and consummated Triune God, and He will be everything to them in His all-inclusive Christ (Rev. 21:2, 11, 23).

2. The Triune God will reign on the earth through such an organism in the new universe (11:15; 22:1-5).

**II. God created a corporate man to express Himself with His image and to represent Him by exercising His dominion over all the earth (Gen. 1:26-28):**

A. God's intention in giving man dominion is to subdue God's enemy, Satan, who rebelled against
God; to recover the earth, which was usurped by
Satan; and to exercise God's authority over the
earth in order that the kingdom of God may come
to the earth, the will of God may be done on the
earth, and the glory of God may be manifested on
the earth (Matt. 6:10, 13b; Rev. 11:15).

*Day 2*

B. Man is especially related to the earth, and the
area where God desires man to rule is the earth;
God needs man to recover the earth from the
usurping hand of Satan, causing Satan to suffer
loss on the earth (Gen. 1:26-28; Psa. 8:1).

C. God's intention that man would express God in
His image and represent God with His dominion
is fulfilled not in Adam as the first man, the old
man, but in Christ as the second man, the new
man, comprising Christ Himself as the Head and
the church as His Body (Eph. 1:22-23; 2:15; 4:15-
16, 24; Col. 3:10-11).

*Day 3*

D. The Lord Jesus, the King, taught us to pray, saying, "Your kingdom come; Your will be done, as in
heaven, so also on earth" (Matt. 6:10):

  1. The kingdom is a realm in which God exercises His authority so that He can express
  His glory (v. 13).

  2. After the rebellion of Satan, the earth fell
  under his usurping hand; thus, the will of God
  could not be done on earth as in heaven;
  hence, God created man with the intention of
  recovering the earth for Himself (Ezek. 28:17;
  Isa. 14:13-15; Gen. 1:26-28).

  3. After the fall of man, Christ came to bring the
  heavenly rule to earth so that the earth would
  be recovered for God's interest and so that the
  will of God could be done on earth as in heaven
  (Matt. 2:2; 27:11; 4:17; 12:28).

  4. The church brings in the kingdom; the work
  of the church is to bring in the kingdom of

God (6:10; 12:22-29; Rev. 11:15; 12:10).

    5.  The believers must pray for the coming of the kingdom until the earth is fully recovered for God's will in the coming kingdom age (Matt. 18:18-19).

*Day 4*  **III. The book of Psalms unveils the recovery of the earth through God's reigning in Christ and His kingdom (2:8-9; 22:27-28; 48:1-2; 72:8, 19; 93:1; 97:1; 145:1, 11-13):**

  A.  Christ will set up His universal kingdom with the nations as His inheritance and the ends of the earth as His possession; He will rule the nations with an iron rod (2:8-9; Rev. 11:15).

  B.  In Psalm 8 the name of the incarnated, crucified, resurrected, ascended, and exalted Jesus is excellent in the earth according to the divine revelation.

  C.  The church ushers in Christ's kingdom for Christ to rule over the nations (22:27-28):

    1.  The church, produced by Christ's resurrection, is the reality of the kingdom and a precursor to the manifestation of the kingdom in the millennium (Matt. 16:18-19; Rom. 14:17).

    2.  Jehovah as Christ will rule over the nations in the millennial kingdom (Psa. 22:28; 2:8-9; Rev. 19:15; 20:4, 6).

*Day 5*  D.  In Psalm 24 Christ is the King who will regain the entire earth through the church, His Body:

    1.  At His second coming Christ will take possession of the earth, which has been given to Him as His possession (2:8; Rev. 10:1-2).

    2.  He will establish God's kingdom on the whole earth, thus recovering God's right over the earth, which has been usurped by His enemy, Satan (Dan. 2:34-35; Rev. 11:15).

  E.  When the church is enlarged to a city, in which we enjoy God as our everything, God will subdue the peoples and the nations through the city and rule over all the earth in Christ as the great King (Psa. 46:4, 10; 47:2; 48:1-2).

F.  Psalm 89 unveils God's intention that Christ, His Anointed, would possess the entire earth (vv. 3-4, 19-29, 34-37):

1.  In verses 19 and 20 Christ, the unique One in God's record (87:6), has become God's Holy One, God's mighty One, God's anointed One (Acts 2:27; Isa. 9:6; Matt. 1:16).

2.  He has become the Firstborn and "the highest of the kings of the earth" (Psa. 89:27; Rom. 8:29; Rev. 1:5a).

3.  God will extend the territory of this unique One so that He will possess the entire earth, setting "His hand on the sea / And His right hand on the rivers" (Psa. 89:25; cf. Rev. 10:1-2).

4.  The fact that Christ's territory will be extended to all the rivers indicates that Christ will possess the whole earth (Psa. 2:8).

*Day 6*

G.  Psalms 93—101 shout joyfully that God will recover His full title and right over the whole earth through the reign of Christ:

1.  These psalms reveal that Christ's reign is through the house and city of God (93:5; 96:6; 99:1-2; 100:1-4; 101:8).

2.  God has the right over the earth because the earth with all its fullness—all the different peoples of all races and colors—was created by Him (93:1):

a.  Thus, He is the Possessor of the earth and holds the title deed (24:1).

b.  He has the full right to claim the earth, and He will do it through the reign of Christ (2:8; Rev. 10:2; 11:15).

3.  Psalm 95 unveils that Jehovah as Christ is a great King who possesses the earth (vv. 4-7).

4.  Psalm 96:3-13 indicates that Jehovah as Christ will come to judge the earth, the world, and the peoples with righteousness and truth and that He will reign over the nations; the word *peoples* in verses 3, 5, 7, 10, and 13 indicates that people

of every race and color will be judged by Christ in His reign over the nations (cf. Matt. 25:31-46).

5. According to Psalm 97:1-2, 4-6, 8-9, and 11, Jehovah as Christ will reign, and because of this the earth will be glad and rejoice.

H. In Psalm 145:1 and 11-13 David praises God for His reigning in Christ and His kingdom (cf. 1 Chron. 29:10-13).

## Morning Nourishment

Luke  ...All the things written in the Law of Moses and the
24:44  Prophets and Psalms concerning Me must be fulfilled.
Gen.  And God said, Let Us make man in Our image, accord-
1:26  ing to Our likeness; and let them have dominion...
Rev.  ...The kingdom of the world has become the *king-*
11:15  *dom* of our Lord and of His Christ, and He will reign
        forever and ever.
19:10  ...The testimony of Jesus is the spirit of the prophecy.

Revelation 19:10 says that the spirit of the prophecy of the
book of Revelation is the testimony of Jesus. Based upon this
principle we can say that the spirit, the reality, the characteristic,
of the divine revelation in the book of Psalms is Christ (Luke
24:44) as the centrality and universality of the eternal economy of
God. For this, He is firstly the embodiment of the Triune God,
then the house, the habitation, of God (signified by the temple),
the kingdom of God (signified by the city of Jerusalem), and the
Ruler of the entire earth from the house of God and in the kingdom of God. Thus, He is all in all in the entire universe. Such a
divine revelation is the same as what is revealed in the entire
Holy Scriptures. The only particular point of the divine revelation
in the book of Psalms is that such a high revelation, even the
highest peak of the divine revelation, is prophesied in the expres-
sions of the sentiments of the ancient godly saints. So it is mixed
with their comfort in sufferings and the cultivation of godliness,
yet the center and the reality, the spirit, of this highest revelation
is not the comfort in sufferings nor the cultivation of godliness. It
is the Christ of God, who is all in all according to God's desire and
for God's good pleasure. (*Life-study of the Psalms,* p. 512)

## Today's Reading

The consummation of this highest divine revelation is the
city of New Jerusalem as a sign of the habitation, the tabernacle,
of God (Rev. 21:1-3), through which the Triune God is manifested and expressed in the all-inclusive Christ.

C. God desires to have an organic habitation on earth, and this habitation is the aggregate of the living saints gained by God through the terminating death and germinating resurrection of the all-inclusive Christ. They will be the eternal manifestation and expression of the processed and consummated Triune God, and He will be everything to them in His all-inclusive Christ.

2. The Triune God will reign on the new earth through such an organism in the new universe. This is the spirit, the extract, of the book of Psalms. (*Life-study of the Psalms,* pp. 512-513)

God created a corporate man not only to express Himself with His image but also to represent Him by exercising His dominion over all things. God's intention in giving man dominion is (1) to subdue God's enemy, Satan, who rebelled against God; (2) to recover the earth, which was usurped by Satan; and (3) to exercise God's authority over the earth in order that the kingdom of God may come to the earth, the will of God may be done on the earth, and the glory of God may be manifested on the earth (Matt. 6:10, 13b).

C. God's intention that man would express God in His image and represent God with His dominion is fulfilled not in Adam as the first man (1 Cor. 15:45a), the old man (Rom. 6:6), but in Christ as the second man (1 Cor. 15:47b and footnote 2), the new man (Eph. 2:15 and footnote 8), comprising Christ Himself as the Head and the church as His Body (Eph. 1:22-23; 1 Cor. 12:12 and footnote 2; Col. 3:10-11 and footnote 11[9]). It is fully fulfilled in the overcoming believers, who live Christ for His corporate expression (Phil. 1:19-26) and will have authority over the nations and reign as co-kings with Christ in the millennium (Rev. 2:26-27; 20:4, 6). It will ultimately be fulfilled in the New Jerusalem, which will express God's image, having His glory and bearing His appearance (Rev. 4:3a; 21:11, 18a), and also exercise God's divine authority to maintain God's dominion over the entire universe for eternity (Rev. 21:24; 22:5). (Gen. 1:26, footnote 5)

*Further Reading: Life-study of the Psalms,* msg. 45

## *Enlightenment and inspiration:* _____

_____
_____
_____

## *Morning Nourishment*

**Gen.**  **...Let Us make man in Our image, according to Our**
**1:26-28**  **likeness; and let them have dominion...over all the**
**earth and over every creeping thing that creeps upon**
**the earth. And God created man in His own image; in**
**the image of God He created him; male and female He**
**created them. And God blessed them; and God said to**
**them, Be fruitful and multiply, and fill the earth and**
**subdue it, and have dominion...over every living thing**
**that moves upon the earth.**

Why did God create man? What was His purpose in creating
man? God has given us the answer to these questions in Genesis
1:26 and 27....From these verses we see the man that God
desired. God desired a ruling man, a man who would rule upon
this earth; then He would be satisfied.

God...created man in His own image. God wanted a man like
Himself....We notice here something quite remarkable. Verse 26
says, "Let us make man in *Our* image, according to *Our* likeness..."; but verse 27 says, "And God created man in *His* own
image; in the image of God He created him; male and female He
created them."...How can we explain this? It is because there are
three in the Godhead—the Father, the Son, and the Spirit, yet
only one has the image in the Godhead—the Son....From this we
ascertain that Adam was made in the image of the Lord Jesus.
Adam did not precede the Lord Jesus; the Lord Jesus preceded
him. When God created Adam, He created him in the image of the
Lord Jesus. It is for this reason it says "in His image" rather than
"in Their image." (*The Glorious Church,* pp. 5-6)

## *Today's Reading*

It is by man that God's plan is fulfilled, and through man His
own need is met. What, then, does God require from the man
whom He created? It is that man should rule. When God created
man, He did not predestine man to fall. Man's fall is in chapter
three of Genesis, not chapter one. In God's plan to create man,

He did not predestine man to sin, neither did He foreordain redemption. We are not minimizing the importance of redemption, but only saying that redemption was not foreordained by God. If it were, then man would have to sin. God did not foreordain this. In God's plan to create man, man was ordained to rule. This is revealed to us in Genesis 1:26. Here God unveils to us His desire and tells us the secret of His plan.

Perhaps some may ask why God has such a purpose. It is because an angel of light rebelled against God before man's creation and became the devil: Satan sinned and fell; the Daystar became the enemy of God (Isa. 14:12-15). God, therefore, withdrew His authority from the enemy and put it, instead, into the hand of man. The reason God created man is that man may rule in the place of Satan. What abounding grace we see in God's creation of man!

Not only does God desire that man should rule, but He marks out a specific area for man to rule. We see this in Genesis 1:26: "Let them have dominion over the fish of the sea and over the birds of heaven and over the cattle and over all the earth...." "All the earth" is the domain of man's rule. Not only did God give man dominion over the fish of the sea, the birds of the heavens, and the cattle, but He further required that man should rule over "all the earth." The area where God desired man to rule is the earth. Man is especially related to the earth. Not only in His plan to create man was God's attention focused upon the earth, but after God made man, He clearly told him that he was to rule over the earth....What God emphasized [in verses 27 and 28] is that man should "fill the earth" and "subdue it"; it is of secondary importance that man should have dominion over the fish of the sea, the birds of heaven, and every living thing on the earth. Man's dominion over these other things is an accessory; the main subject is the earth. (*The Glorious Church,* pp. 7-8)

*Further Reading: The Glorious Church,* ch. 1; *Life-study of Genesis,*
   msg. 6

## *Enlightenment and inspiration:* _____

_____
_____
_____

## Morning Nourishment

Matt. You then pray in this way: Our Father who is in the
6:9-10 heavens, Your name be sanctified; Your kingdom come;
Your will be done, as in heaven, *so* also on earth.
   13 ...For Yours is the kingdom and the power and the
glory forever. Amen.

After the rebellion of Satan (Ezek. 28:17; Isa. 14:13-15), the
earth fell into his usurping hand. Thus, the will of God could not
be done on earth as in heaven. Hence, God created man with the
intention of recovering the earth for Himself (Gen. 1:26-28).
After the fall of man, Christ came to bring the heavenly rule to
earth so that the earth could be recovered for God's interest, so
that the will of God could be done on earth as in heaven. This is
why the new King established the kingdom of the heavens with
His followers. The kingdom people must pray for this until the
earth is fully recovered for God's will in the coming kingdom age.
(Matt. 6:10, footnote 1)

## Today's Reading

We see then that the earth is the center of all problems. God
contends for the earth....According to the meaning of the original
language, [in Matt. 6:9-10] the phrase "as in heaven, so also on earth"
is common to all three clauses, not only to the last clause....This
prayer reveals that there is no problem with "heaven"; the problem
is with the "earth." After the fall of man, God spoke to the serpent,
"Upon your stomach you will go, / And dust you will eat / All the
days of your life" (Gen. 3:14). This meant that the earth would be
the serpent's sphere, the place upon which he would creep. The
realm of Satan's work is not heaven, but earth. If the kingdom of
God is to come, then Satan must be cast out. If God's will is to be
done, it must be done on earth. If God's name is to be sanctified, it
must be sanctified on earth. All the problems are on the earth.

Some may ask: Why doesn't God Himself cast Satan into the
bottomless pit or the lake of fire? Our answer is: God can do it,
but He does not want to do it Himself. We do not know why He
will not do it Himself, but we do know how He is going to do it.

God wants to use man to deal with His enemy, and He created man for this purpose. God wants the creature to deal with the creature. He wants His creature *man* to deal with His fallen creature *Satan* in order to bring the earth back to God. The man whom He created is being used by Him for this purpose.

We must distinguish the difference between the work of saving souls and the work of God. Many times the work of saving souls is not necessarily the work of God. Saving souls solves the problem of man, but the work of God requires that man exercise authority to have dominion over all things created by Him. God needs an authority in His creation, and He has chosen man to be that authority....We are on this earth not merely for man's need but even more for God's need....When God created man, He spoke of what He needed. He revealed His need to have man rule and reign over all His creation and proclaim His triumph. Ruling for God is not a small thing; it is a great matter. God needs men whom He can trust and who will not fail Him. This is God's work, and this is what God desires to obtain. (*The Glorious Church,* pp. 9-11)

The church is responsible for working together with God to bring in His kingdom. At the same time, God's kingdom will appear physically only at the end time. For this reason, the church has to pay attention to the end time. The end has to come before the kingdom can come. Hence, in order for the kingdom to come, the end must first come. The end itself is not related to the church, but it has much to do with the work of the church.

The gospel of the kingdom of heaven is nothing but God (who rules in heaven today) ruling the earth and completely casting away the ruler of this present world together with his messengers and evil spirits, so that man (that is, Christ and the church) can rule on God's behalf. (*The Collected Works of Watchman Nee,* vol. 8, pp. 16, 18)

*Further Reading: The Collected Works of Watchman Nee,* vol. 8, pp. 15-21; vol. 44, pp. 777-781; *Authority and Submission,* ch. 6

***Enlightenment and inspiration:*** _____

_____

_____

## Morning Nourishment

Psa. Ask of Me, and I will give the nations as Your inher-
2:8-9 itance and the limits of the earth as Your possession. You will break them with an iron rod...

8:1-2 O Jehovah our Lord, how excellent is Your name in
all the earth, You who have set Your glory over the
heavens! Out of the mouths of babes and sucklings
You have established strength because of Your
adversaries, to stop the enemy and the avenger.

Eventually, Christ will rule the nations in His kingdom with
an iron rod (Psa. 2:9; Rev. 2:26-27). There is a marvelous sequence
in Psalm 2 revealing the steps of Christ in God's economy....In
Psalm 2 we see His being anointed in His divinity and humanity,
His death, His resurrection, and His ascension with His en-
thronement. God installed Him as King, enthroning Him to give
Him all the nations with the limits of the earth. This is to set up a
universal kingdom for Christ. Then Christ will rule the nations
with an iron rod. (*Life-study of the Psalms*, p. 36)

In Psalm 8, the name of the incarnated, crucified, resurrected, ascended, and exalted Jesus (Phil. 2:5-11) is excellent in
the earth according to the divine revelation, and the Lord's glory
is above the heavens in the sight of David. In this psalm the
earth is linked to the heavens and the heavens are brought
down to the earth, making the earth and the heavens one (Gen.
28:12 and footnote 2). (Psa. 8:1, footnote 2)

## Today's Reading

Psalm 8 shows that God's purpose and plan have never
changed. After the fall, God's will and requirement for man
remained the same without any alteration. His will in Genesis 1,
when He created man, still holds good, even though man has
sinned and fallen. Even though Psalm 8 was written after man's
fall, the psalmist was able to praise; his eyes were still set upon
Genesis 1. The Holy Spirit did not forget Genesis 1, the Son did
not forget Genesis 1, nor did God Himself forget Genesis 1.

The expression "in all the earth" [in Psalm 8:1] is the same as in Genesis 1:26....[In Psalm 8:2]...babes and sucklings refer to man, and the emphasis in this verse is upon God using man to deal with the enemy. The Lord Jesus quoted this verse in Matthew 21:16: "Out of the mouth of infants and sucklings You have perfected praise." These words mean that the enemy may do all he can, but it is not necessary for God Himself to deal with him. God will use babes and sucklings to deal with him. What can babes and sucklings do?...God's desire is to obtain men who are able to praise; those who can praise are those who can deal with the enemy.

In God's view the earth can still be restored, the position given to man by God still exists, and His commitment to man to destroy the work of the devil still remains....Is man worthy? Certainly not! But since God's purpose is for man to rule, man will surely rule....Even after man fell, God's will toward man remained the same. God still requires man to overthrow the power of Satan. Oh, what an unchangeable God He is! His way is unswerving and utterly straightforward. We must realize that God can never be overthrown. (*The Glorious Church,* pp. 12-14)

Christ's church ushers in His kingdom for Him to rule over the nations. Psalm 22:27-28 says, "All the ends of the earth / Will remember and return to Jehovah, / And all families of the nations / Will worship before You; / For the kingdom is Jehovah's, / And He rules among the nations." Christ has the kingdom, and He will rule among the nations.

The church ushers in the kingdom. Actually, the church is the reality of the kingdom and a precursor of the manifestation of the kingdom. Today the church is the kingdom. Romans 14:17 says the church life is the kingdom life, the kingdom of God.... Today's church life is a miniature, a precursor, of the coming kingdom of one thousand years. The church is produced by the resurrection of Christ, and the kingdom will be ushered in by the church. (*Life-study of the Psalms,* p. 135)

*Further Reading: Life-study of the Psalms,* msgs. 3, 10

## *Enlightenment and inspiration:* _____

_____
_____
_____

## *Morning Nourishment*

Psa. The earth is Jehovah's, and its fullness, the habitable
24:1 land and those who dwell in it.
47:2 For Jehovah Most High is awesome: a great King
over all the earth.

[Psalm 24:1] means that the Lord has the right, the title, to this
earth. "It is He who founded it upon the seas / And established it
upon the streams" (v. 2). He has established it, so it is His. Apparently, the earth today is not the Lord's. Even when this psalm was
written, the earth was apparently not the Lord's. But have you realized that on this earth there was at least a mountain, which was
called His holy mountain, and at least that mountain was His?
Thus, verse 3 says, "Who may ascend the mountain of Jehovah?"
The earth is the Lord's, but actually, today the earth is not the
Lord's. Yet on this earth there is at least a mountain, at least a spot,
which is the Lord's.

Verse 3 asks, "Who may ascend the mountain of Jehovah, /
And who may stand in His holy place?" The answer is, Christ and
His brothers. The church is a mountain which is occupied by the
Lord today as the very steppingstone, the beachhead, for the Lord
to come back. The earth is the Lord's, but today the earth is
usurped; yet in this usurped earth there is a spot, a mountain,
which is the steppingstone for the Lord to return to take the
whole earth. (*Christ and the Church Revealed and Typified in the
Psalms*, p. 56)

## *Today's Reading*

In the background of Psalm 24, the mountain of Zion was
there, but the Ark was missing. Now the Ark is coming in; Christ
is coming in. And while the Ark was entering, David said, "Lift up
your heads, O gates; / And be lifted up, O long enduring doors; /
And the King of glory will come in" [v. 7]. We may be the mountain
of Zion, we may be the local church, but the King of glory is not so
absolutely within. We need to be open, we need to be lifted up, to
let the King of glory come in all the way. Then the church will be

the steppingstone, the beachhead, for the Lord to return and possess the earth....If He can fully possess this area, He can return to take over the whole earth. This is the thought, the deep thought, of Psalm 24. Praise the Lord!

Psalm 47:2-3 says, "Jehovah Most High is awesome: / A great King over all the earth. / He subdues people under us, / And nations under our feet." These are all God's doings in Christ through the city, the enlarged church. When the church is enlarged as a city, God will subdue the peoples through the city and rule over all the earth in Christ as a great King. Without such a church it would be difficult for God to accomplish this. It is the church enlarged as a city that will bring the entire earth under God's authority and kingship in Christ. (*Christ and the Church Revealed and Typified in the Psalms,* pp. 57-58, 90)

Psalm 89...unveils the intention of God for Christ, His Anointed, to possess the entire earth....The prayer in Psalm 89 is concerned with Christ, the unique One. God cares for this One, the One who was born in Zion, not for our sufferings.

The unique One in God's record in Psalm 87 has become God's anointed One, God's Holy One, God's mighty One, in Psalm 89. He has become the Firstborn and "the highest of the kings of the earth" (v. 27). His throne will be like the sun before God; it will be established forever like the moon (vv. 36-37). God will establish His seed forever and "His throne as the days of heaven" (v. 29). God will extend the territory of this unique One so that He will possess the entire earth, setting "His hand on the sea / And His right hand on the rivers" (v. 25)....The word "rivers" indicates that all the earth will belong to Christ. All the parts of the earth are signified by their rivers, such as Egypt by the Nile and Babylon by the Euphrates. That Christ's territory will be extended to all the rivers indicates that Christ will possess all the parts of the earth and that He will therefore possess the whole earth. (*Life-study of the Psalms,* p. 394)

*Further Reading: Christ and the Church Revealed and Typified in the Psalms,* chs. 5-6, 8, 15; *Life-study of the Psalms,* msgs. 11, 13, 19, 34

### *Enlightenment and inspiration:* _____

_____

_____

_____

## Morning Nourishment

**Psa.** ...Jehovah...is coming to judge the earth; He will
**96:13** judge the world with righteousness, and the peoples with His truth.
**97:1** Jehovah reigns! Let the earth be glad; let the many
islands rejoice.
**145:11-13** They will speak of the glory of Your kingdom...to
make known...the glorious splendor of Your king-
dom. Your kingdom is an eternal kingdom...

Psalms 93 through 101 show us that God will recover His full title and right over the earth through the reign of Christ.... [These
Psalms] shout joyfully that God will recover His title and right over
the whole earth. God has the right over the earth because the earth
with all its fullness—all the different peoples, regardless of race or
color—was created by Him. Thus, He is the Possessor of the earth
and holds the title deed....According to Psalm 101, Christ will
reign and judge in lovingkindness and justice.

Psalm 94:15a says, "Judgment will return unto righteousness."
This indicates that on earth today judgment has gone astray from
righteousness, but when Christ comes back to reign, He will bring
in justice and will cause judgment to return to righteousness.
Christ is with us in the church, but today's world is without Christ,
and for this reason the world is evil, dark, and sinful. However, the
coming reign of Christ will make a great difference throughout
the earth. Instead of injustice and unrighteousness, there will be
justice and righteousness. (*Life-study of the Psalms*, p. 408)

## Today's Reading

In Psalm 96:3-13 we see that Christ will come to judge the earth,
the world, and the peoples with righteousness and truth and that
He will reign over the nations. The word "peoples"...indicates that
people of every race and color will be judged by Him. In verse 13 the
psalmist concludes by saying that Jehovah "is coming to judge the
earth; / He will judge the world with righteousness, / And the peoples with His truth." This surely reveals that God will recover His
title and right over the earth through the reign of Christ.

According to Psalm 97…Christ will reign, and the earth will be glad and rejoicing. Today the earth is not pleasant, and thus the inhabitants of the earth are not glad. But when Christ reigns, the earth will be glad and will rejoice.

Psalm 100 opens with a charge to all the earth: "Make a joyful noise to Jehovah, all the earth" (v. 1).…When we are joyful we will shout, and to shout is surely to make a noise. Sometimes in our meetings we should make a joyful noise to the Lord, praising Him and shouting "Hallelujah!" This will make the Lord happy, and it will put the devil and the demons to shame. When we are silent, we are deadened, but when we praise the Lord with a joyful noise, we are strengthened.

Psalms 140 through 144 issue in the extolling and praising of God.…In [Psalm 145:10-13] David goes on to extol and praise God for the glory of His kingdom. In verse 12 he speaks of the "glorious splendor" of God's kingdom, and in verse 13 he declares, "Your kingdom is an eternal kingdom, / And Your dominion is throughout all generations." (*Life-study of the Psalms,* pp. 411-412, 505).

The main point of Psalm 146 [is that]…"Jehovah will reign forever…O Zion" (v. 10). Zion is the city, and the Lord's reigning is for the earth.

In Psalm 147 we have praise for God's building of Jerusalem: "Hallelujah! / For it is good to sing psalms to our God; / For it is pleasant; praise is fitting. / Jehovah builds up Jerusalem" (vv. 1-2a).

[The] last five psalms are all psalms of praise for the house, the city and the earth, and mostly for the city, because [the book of Psalms] has come to its ultimate consummation. Revelation 21 describes the final scene in the entire Bible—it is a revelation of the city for the earth, the New Jerusalem and the earth, with all the kings bringing their glory into it. Eventually, we just have the city and the earth. (*Christ and the Church Revealed and Typified in the Psalms,* pp. 219, 221)

*Further Reading: Life-study of the Psalms,* msgs. 35-37, 44; *Christ and the Church Revealed and Typified in the Psalms,* chs. 17, 23-24

***Enlightenment and inspiration:*** _____
_____
_____
_____

### *Hymns,* #1224

1   We from the law to Christ have turned;
    To trust in Him by grace we've learned.
    And since His glory we've discerned
      We only care for Christ!

    We only care for Christ!
    We only care for Christ!
    And since His glory we've discerned
    We only care for Christ!

2   Christ brings us to God's house to dwell,
    Where all day long His praises swell.
    O hallelujah! None can tell
      How lovely is God's house!

    How lovely is God's house!
    How lovely is God's house!
    O hallelujah! None can tell
    How lovely is God's house!

3   The house enlarged the city is;
    The joy of all the nations 'tis,
    The place for God to rule is this
      On Zion's holy hill.

    On Zion's holy hill,
    On Zion's holy hill,
    The place for God to rule is this
    On Zion's holy hill.

4   From Zion Christ will take the earth
    And reign and fill its souls with mirth.
    All nations will proclaim His worth,
      Break forth and sing for joy.

    Break forth and sing for joy,
    Break forth and sing for joy,
    All nations will proclaim His worth,
    Break forth and sing for joy.

5    Christ—house—the city—earth, we see;
     Thus God's great plan fulfilled will be.
     O brothers, let us utterly
        Be one with Him for this.

        Be one with Him for this,
        Be one with Him for this,
        O brothers, let us utterly
        Be one with Him for this.

*Composition for prophecy with main point and sub-points:* _____

_____
_____
_____
_____
_____
_____
_____
_____
_____
_____
_____
_____
_____
_____
_____
_____
_____
_____
_____
_____
_____
_____
_____
_____
_____
_____
_____
_____
_____

*Offering the Consummate Praise to God
for the Recovery of Christ, the House,
the City, and the Earth*

Scripture Reading: Psa. 146–150; 2:6-7; 27:4; 48:1-2; 72:8;
22:22b; Heb. 2:12b; 13:15

*Day 1*  **I. Praise is the highest work carried out by God's
children (Psa. 119:164; 34:1):**
  A. The highest expression of a saint's spiritual life is
  his praise to God (146:2; Heb. 13:15; Rev. 5:9-13;
  19:1-6):
    1. The Christian life soars through praises (Acts
    16:19-34). *Paul + Silas praying + praising at midnight*
    2. To praise is to transcend everything to touch
    the Lord (Rev. 14:1-3; 15:2-4).
  B. Spiritual victory does not depend on warfare—it
  depends on praise (2 Chron. 20:20-22). *singing + praising before the army*
  C. We need to see that God is above everything and
  that He is worthy of our praise (Psa. 18:3; 1 Chron.
  29:10-13; Rev. 4:1-3, 10-11; 5:6, 9-13).

*Day 2*  **II. Exodus 15:1-18 is a song of praise to God for
His salvation and His victory, leading to God's
habitation and God's kingdom:**
  *In v.1-12 God praised God for His salvation + His victory. I will sing to Jah for He has triumphed. Jah is my God + song. He has become my salvation. This is my God + I will praise*
  A. Salvation is related to God's people, and victory, to
  His enemy; at the time God defeated the enemy,
  He also saved His people (cf. Heb. 2:14-15). *Thru death He might destroy Him who has might of death + might release + those who the fear of death thru all their life were held in slavery*
  B. Exodus 15:13 speaks of God's habitation, even
  though the temple as God's dwelling place was not
  built until centuries later.
  C. Verse 18 refers to the kingdom: "Jehovah shall
  reign forever and ever":
    1. God's habitation, God's house, brings in God's
    kingdom, God's reign.
    2. Today the church is first God's house and then
    His kingdom; the church brings the kingdom
    to the earth (1 Tim. 3:15; Rom. 14:17; Eph.
    2:19; Matt. 16:18-19).

3. Exodus 15:1-18 indicates that the goal of God's salvation is the building of His dwelling place for the establishing of His kingdom, and for this we, like Moses and the children of Israel, should praise the Lord (cf. Rev. 15:2-4).

*Day 3* **III. The book of Psalms is a book of praise; in the Psalms we find the greatest and highest praise:**

A. The following verses reveal crucial aspects of praise in the Psalms: *You have turned my mourning into dancing*

1. "O Jehovah my God, I will praise You forever" (30:12b). *Believe this will be your future*

2. "Every day I will bless You, / And I will praise Your name forever and ever" (145:2). *for His reigning in c + His Kingdom*

3. "I will bless Jehovah at all times; / His praise will continually be in my mouth" (34:1). *not heart*

4. "I will praise Jehovah while I live; / I will sing psalms to my God while I yet have being" (146:2). *Praise Jeh for His reigning in Christ thru him*

5. "Then they believed His words; / They sang His praise" (106:12). *If we believe we will praise*

6. "Because Your lovingkindness is better than life, / My lips praise You" (63:3). *soul – sweetness, tender love, affectionate care*

7. "I will cause Your name to be remembered in all generations; / Therefore the peoples will praise You forever and ever" (45:17). *not again  overcoming suffer  nations  in place of fathers*

8. "Great is Jehovah, / And much to be praised / In the city of our God, / In His holy mountain" (48:1). *In strong + enlarged city old God be open + greatly praised  will be upon you  You will see  when praised in all to u*

9. "Praise befits You, O God, in Zion" (65:1). *awaits  for reigning in N then*

10. "That the name of Jehovah may be declared in Zion, / And His praise, in Jerusalem" (102:21). *when people gather together sk to come*

11. "Let the high praises of God be in their throats, / And a two-edged sword in their hand, / To execute vengeance on the nations / And punishment among the peoples; / To bind their kings with fetters / And their nobles with chains of iron; / To execute upon them the judgment written. / This honor is for all His faithful ones. / Hallelujah!" (149:6-9).

*thru est. + restored Zion all nations + K will be brought into praise + worship of Jeh*

12. "You are holy, You who sit enthroned / Upon the praises of Israel" (22:3).

*Day 4*

B. The praise of Jehovah in Psalms 103—106 issues in Hallelujahs, beginning in 104:35, because the earth has been fully recovered by God and brought under the reign of Christ in His kingdom (cf. Rev. 19:1-6; 11:15).

C. Psalms 146 through 150—the Hallelujah psalms— are the consummate praise:

1. Psalm 146 concerns the praising of Jehovah for His reigning from Zion (v. 10).

2. Psalm 147 is a praise to Jehovah for the rebuilding of Jerusalem.

3. Psalm 148 is a praise to Jehovah for His exalted name and for His transcending majesty (v. 13).

4. Psalm 149 is a praise to Jehovah for His taking pleasure in His people, Israel, and His adorning of the lowly with salvation (v. 4).

5. Psalm 150 is on praising Jehovah God:

   a. This psalm is a concluding charge to everything that has breath to praise God (v. 6).

   b. Psalm 150 is not only the conclusion of the Psalms—it is the consummation of the entire Bible, for the Psalms are a miniature of the whole Bible.

   c. The consummate praise in Psalm 150 corresponds with the praise at the end of Revelation (Rev. 19:1-6).

*Day 5*

D. The Psalms reveal that the Lord has turned us from the law to Christ, that Christ has brought us to the house, that He is enlarging the house into the city, and that from the city He will gain the earth; then God's purpose will be fulfilled, and we will declare, "O Jehovah our Lord, / How excellent is Your name / In all the earth!" (2:6-7; 27:4; 48:1-2; 72:8; 8:9).

IV. **In the church life and in our personal life, we need to offer consummate praise to God (22:22b; Heb. 2:12b; 13:15):**

A. "In the midst of the assembly I will praise You" (Psa. 22:22b):
  1. The assembly here refers to the church, in which the resurrected Christ sings hymns of praise to God the Father.
  2. This is the firstborn Son's praising of the Father within the Father's many sons in the church meetings (Heb. 2:10, 12):
    a. When we, the many sons of God, meet as the church and praise the Father, the first-born Son praises the Father in our praising; He praises within us and with us through our praising (v. 12b).
    b. The church on earth today is one corporate Body with the firstborn Son of God (Rom. 8:29; 12:4-5):
      1) To gain more of the firstborn Son, we need to praise the Father; the more we praise the Father, the more we gain the firstborn Son.
      2) The more we sing, the more we will enjoy His singing in our singing; the best way to cooperate with Christ and to have Him work together with us is by singing praises to the Father (Heb. 2:12).

*Day 6*

B. "Through Him then let us offer up a sacrifice of praise continually to God, that is, the fruit of lips confessing His name" (13:15):
  1. When we pass through reproach and suffering, we should continually offer up a sacrifice of praise to God (vv. 12-14).
  2. Since in the church life we enjoy the unchanging Christ as grace and follow Him outside religion, we should offer through Him spiritual sacrifices to God (vv. 8-10, 15):
    a. In the church we should offer up through Christ a sacrifice of praise to God continually (v. 15).
    b. In the church He and we, we and He, praise

the Father together in the mingled spirit
(2:12b; 1 Cor. 6:17):

   1) He, as the life-giving Spirit, praises the
   Father in our spirit, and we, by our spirit,
   praise the Father in His Spirit (15:45b;
   John 4:24; Eph. 2:18; Jude 20-21).

   2) This is the best and highest sacrifice
   that we can offer to God through Him
   (Heb. 2:12b; 13:15; cf. Hosea 14:1-3).

3. Through the Christ whom we have experienced
and enjoyed, we need to offer the sacrifice of
praise to God continually (Heb. 1:2-3; 2:9, 17;
3:1; 4:14; 6:20; 7:25; 8:1; 12:2; 13:8, 15):

   a. The real praise to the Father comes out of
   our experience and enjoyment of Christ in
   our daily life; this is a very pleasing praise
   to the Father, gladdening and rejoicing
   His heart (Eph. 3:8, 17a; John 4:24).

   b. The praises out of our experience and enjoy-
   ment of Christ—the spiritual praises about
   Christ—are the best praise to the Father
   (Psa. 45:1-2; 145:1).

C. "I will praise You, O Lord my God, with all my heart;/
And I will glorify Your name forever" (86:12).

D. "Jehovah will reign forever, / Your God, O Zion,
forever and ever. / Hallelujah!" (146:10).

## Morning Nourishment

**Psa.** **Seven times a day I praise You for Your righteous**
**119:164** **ordinances.**
  **34:1** **I will bless Jehovah at all times; His praise will**
       **continually be in my mouth.**

Praise is the highest work carried out by God's children. We can say that the highest expression of a saint's spiritual life is his praise to God. God's throne is the highest point in the universe, yet He sits "enthroned upon the praises of Israel" (Psa. 22:3). God's name and even God Himself are exalted through praise.

David said in a psalm that he prayed to God three times a day (Psa. 55:17). Yet in another psalm, he said that he praised God *seven* times a day (119:164). David was inspired by the Holy Spirit when he acknowledged the importance of praising....We should praise the Lord all our life. We should sing praises to our God. (Watchman Nee, *Praising,* pp. 1-2)

## Today's Reading

The Christian life soars through praises. To praise is to transcend everything to touch the Lord. This was the pathway our Lord Jesus took when He was on earth. We should take the same way. We should not murmur against heaven when we are under trials. We should soar above the trials. Once we praise, we are above the trials. The more others try to put us down, the more we should rise up before the Lord and say, "I thank You and praise You!" Learn to accept everything. Learn to know that He is God. Learn to know the works of His hands. Nothing can ripen and mature a man like sacrifices of praise. We need to learn not only to accept the discipline of the Holy Spirit but also to praise the discipline of the Holy Spirit. We need to learn not only to accept but also to glory in the Lord's dealing. We need to learn not only to accept the Lord's chastisement but also to accept it willingly with joy. If we do this, a clear and glorious door will be opened to us.

Here we see that spiritual victory does not depend on

warfare but on praising. We need to learn to overcome Satan by our praise. We overcome Satan not only by prayer but also by praise. Many people are conscious of Satan's ferocity and their own weaknesses, and they resolve to struggle and pray. However, we find a very unique principle here: Spiritual victory does not depend on warfare but on praise. God's children often are tempted to think that their problems are too big and that they have to find some way to deal with their problems. They pay much attention to finding a way to overcome. But the more they try to come up with a way, the harder it is for them to overcome. In doing so, they put themselves on Satan's level. They are both in the battle; Satan is fighting on one side, and they are fighting on the other side. It is not easy to win from this position. But 2 Chronicles 20 gives a different picture. On one side was the army, and on the other side was the singing of hymns. These ones either had great faith in God, or they were crazy. Thank God, we are not crazy people. We are those who have faith in God.

Once God's glory fills your eyes, you can believe. Once His glory fills your spirit, you can praise. You have to see that God is above everything and is worthy of your praise. When you praise, Satan flees away. Sometimes we need to pray. But when our prayer reaches the point where we have faith and assurance, we know that the Lord has answered our prayer, and we should praise: "Lord! I thank You! I praise You! This matter is already settled!" Do not wait for the matter to be over before you praise. We have to praise as soon as we believe. Do not wait until the enemy runs away to sing. We have to sing to chase him away. We have to learn to praise by faith. When we praise Him in faith, the enemy will be defeated and driven away. We have to believe before we can praise. First we believe and praise, and then we will experience victory. (Watchman Nee, *Praising,* pp. 23-24, 15-16, 20-21)

*Further Reading: Praising; How to Meet,* chs. 12-13

### *Enlightenment and inspiration:* _____

_____

_____

_____

## Morning Nourishment

**Exo.** **In Your lovingkindness You have led the people**
**15:13** **whom You have redeemed; You have guided them**
**in Your strength to Your holy habitation.**
**17-18** **You will bring them in and plant them in the**
**mountain of Your inheritance, the place, O Jeho-**
**vah, which You have made for Your dwelling, the**
**sanctuary, O Lord, which Your hands have estab-**
**lished. Jehovah shall reign forever and ever.**

*perfect tense.*

In Revelation 5 we read that when Christ ascended to the heavens, the four living creatures and the twenty-four elders sang a new song, saying, "You are worthy..." (v. 9). They did not give a sermon or listen to a message; they just praised, praised, praised! "To the Lamb be the blessing and the honor and the glory and the might forever and ever" (v. 13). And the four living creatures said, "Amen." How good it would be if we could have a meeting just for praising. This kind of praising will simply bring you into an ecstasy; you will be in the third heavens with everything under your feet. (*How to Meet,* p. 116)

## Today's Reading

Immediately after crossing the Red Sea, Moses and the children of Israel sang a song to the Lord (Exo. 15:1-18). This song must have been composed by Moses [cf. Rev. 15:2-4]....The children of Israel sang this song on the shore of the Red Sea; they praised God for victory over the forces of Pharaoh by His triumphant deliverance through the judging waters of the Red Sea. In Revelation 15 a number of overcomers sing this song again on the glassy sea as an indication that they are victorious over the power of Antichrist, who is judged by God with the fire of the glassy sea (Rev. 19:20). In both cases the principle is the same: God's people are saved through the sea, and now they can sing praises to God.

In [Exodus] 15:1-12 the children of Israel praised God's salvation and victory. Salvation is related to God's people, and victory is related to God's enemy. At the same time God defeated the enemy, He also saved His people. How beautiful is the poetic expression of praise concerning this!...Using the perfect tense, verse 13... speaks of God's habitation, even though the temple as God's dwelling place was not built until centuries later.

Verses 14 and 15 say that the peoples will be afraid, that the inhabitants of Philistia will be sorrowful, that the princes of Edom will be amazed, that trembling will take hold of the mighty men of Moab, and that the inhabitants of Canaan will melt away. In poetic form, this is a prophecy that the children of Israel would defeat the Philistines, the descendants of Esau and Moab, and all the Canaanites, and would take possession of the good land.

In verse 17 we are told that the Lord would plant His people in the mountain of His inheritance, in the place which He has made to dwell in. This place is the sanctuary which His hands have established. Pay attention to the phrase "the mountain of Your inheritance." Although we regard the good land as the inheritance of the children of Israel, here Moses speaks of it as the inheritance of God. The children of Israel were to be planted as a living organism on the mountain of God's inheritance. I believe that the mountain here refers to Mount Zion. With respect to God's sanctuary, this verse also uses the perfect tense: "The sanctuary, O Lord, which Your hands have established."

Verse 18 refers to the kingdom: "Jehovah shall reign forever and ever." God's habitation, God's house, brings in God's kingdom. When God has a habitation, a house, on the earth, His kingdom will be established through His house. Today the church is firstly God's house and then His kingdom. The church will bring in His kingdom to the earth (Eph. 2:19-20; Rom. 14:17; Matt. 16:18-19).

[From] Exodus 15:1-18, we realize that the goal of God's salvation is the building of His dwelling place for the establishment of His kingdom....Moses did not enter into the good land, much less see the building of the temple, [but] he could still praise the Lord for His sanctuary, His dwelling place. (*Life-study of Exodus*, pp. 340-341)

*Further Reading: Life-study of Exodus, msg. 29; Experiencing Christ as the Offerings for the Church Meetings, ch. 2*

## *Enlightenment and inspiration:* _____

_____
_____
_____

## Morning Nourishment

Psa. But You are holy, You who sit *enthroned* upon the
22:3 praises of Israel.
102:21 That the name of Jehovah may be declared in Zion,
and His praise, in Jerusalem.

The Bible pays much attention to praise. It is spoken of frequently in the Scriptures. The book of Psalms is full of praises. The book of Psalms is in fact a book of praise in the Old Testament. Many praises are quoted from Psalms....We need to see the significance of praise at the very beginning of our Christian walk. We must praise God unceasingly. (Watchman Nee, *Praising*, pp. 2, 5)

## Today's Reading

[In Psalm 30] David asked God to hear him and be gracious to him to be his help. He also thanked God for turning his mourning into dancing and loosening his sackcloth to gird him with rejoicing, that his glory (spirit) might sing psalms to God without silence and praise God forever (vv. 10-12).

David begins [Psalm 145] by saying, "I will extol You, O my God and King; / And I will bless Your name forever and ever. / Every day I will bless You, / And I will praise Your name forever and ever" (vv. 1-2). Then David extols and praises God for His unsearchable greatness in His goodness (vv. 3-7)....Psalm 145:21 is David's concluding word...."My mouth will speak the praise of Jehovah, / And all flesh will bless His holy name forever and ever."

[In Psalm 34] David blessed and praised God because of God's answer and deliverance (vv. 1-6). In verse 1 he said, "I will bless Jehovah at all times; / His praise will continually be in my mouth." (*Life-study of the Psalms*, pp. 183, 505-506, 202)

There is praise in Psalm 146 for God's reigning in Christ through Zion. "Hallelujah! / Praise Jehovah, O my soul! I will praise Jehovah while I live; / I will sing psalms to my God while I yet have being" (vv. 1-2). Regardless of what kind of being I am, though I am weak or strong, I will still sing praises to God. In verse 10 the psalmist gives the reason for his praise...[and] the main point of Psalm 146. "Jehovah will reign forever...O Zion."

Zion is the city, and the Lord's reigning is for the earth. There is nothing new; there is just praise for the city and for the Lord's reign in the earth. (*Christ and the Church Revealed and Typified in the Psalms,* p. 219)

In Psalm 45:17 the psalmist says, "I will cause Your name to be remembered in all generations; / Therefore the peoples will praise You forever and ever." This reveals that Christ's name will be remembered in all generations through the overcoming saints and that Christ will be praised by the nations through His overcoming and co-reigning saints. (*Life-study of the Psalms,* pp. 267-268)

Now we come to Psalm 48. "Great is Jehovah, / And much to be praised / In the city of our God" (v. 1). Here we reach the climax of the city. Only in the city, only in the strong and enlarged church, could God be great and greatly praised. (*Christ and the Church Revealed and Typified in the Psalms,* p. 91)

In Psalm 65 we first have the psalmist's praise to God for his enjoyment of God in His house (vv. 1-4), and then the psalmist's praise to God for His goodness to the earth for man (vv. 5-13). (*Life-study of the Psalms,* p. 308)

"Praise befits You, O God, in Zion" (65:1). Brothers and sisters, whenever we come together, are we ready to praise? Do we really have some praises [that befit and are] waiting for God? From now on, whenever you come to the meeting, do not bring two ears itching for teachings, but two lips ready for praise. In 2 Timothy 4:3 the apostle Paul said, "The time will come when they will…heap up to themselves teachers, having itching ears." People pile up teachers because of their itching ears. We need praising lips. Whenever we come to the church meetings, we should be prepared to praise. Even before we come, we must compose something concerning the King. Then when we meet, our praise will be waiting for the Lord, waiting for God in Zion. Praise must be waiting for the Lord in the local churches. (*Christ and the Church Revealed and Typified in the Psalms,* p. 102)

*Further Reading: How to Meet,* chs. 14-15

### *Enlightenment and inspiration:* _____

_____

_____

_____

## Morning Nourishment

**Psa.** Let them praise the name of Jehovah, for His name
**148:13** alone is exalted; His glory is above the earth and
the heavens.
**150:1** Hallelujah! Praise God in His sanctuary; praise Him
in the expanse that *manifests* His power.
**6** Let everything that has breath praise Jehovah.
Hallelujah!

Psalms 103—106 are the praising of Jehovah, who has recovered the title and the right over the whole earth through the reign of Christ. In these four psalms there is a narration of God's history....Psalm 103 speaks of God's history in His lovingkindness and compassions in His forgiving of sins, healing, redeeming, and caring for His people. This is the first part of God's history. (Psa. 103:1, footnote 1)

## Today's Reading

Because each of [the last five psalms, Psalms 146 through 150] begins and ends with the word "Hallelujah," these five psalms are called Hallelujah psalms. The Septuagint says that Psalms 146 to 149 were written by Haggai and Zechariah after their return from captivity. The return of God's people from captivity was a great release and restoration.

Psalm 146 is on praising Jehovah for His reigning from Zion.... Verses 3 through 5 are a praise to Jehovah for His being the help of His saints....Verse 10 concludes with the declaration that Jehovah will reign forever and ever....Psalm 147 is on praising Jehovah for the rebuilding of Jerusalem. Verse 2a says, "Jehovah builds up Jerusalem."...Psalm 148 is on praising Jehovah for His exalted name and for His transcending majesty....In verses 1 through 6 all the heavenly things and persons are charged to praise Jehovah from the heavens. Concerning this, verse 5 says, "Let them praise the name of Jehovah; / For He commanded, and they were created."...Verses 7 through 13 continue by saying that all the earthly things and persons are to praise Jehovah from the earth.

Concerning this verse 13 says, "Let them praise the name of Jehovah, / For His name alone is exalted; / His glory is above the earth
and the heavens."…According to verse 14, all His people, His faithful
ones, the children of Israel, a people near to Him, are to praise Him.

Psalm 149 is on praising Jehovah for His pleasure in His people, Israel, and His adornment of the lowly with salvation.…Verse
1 speaks of singing a new song to Jehovah and His praise in the
congregation of His faithful ones.…Verse 2 says, "Let Israel
rejoice in his Maker; / Let the children of Zion exult in their King."
Verse 3 speaks of praising His name with dancing and of singing
psalms to Him with the tambourine and the lyre.

Psalm 150 is a psalm on praising Jehovah God.…Verse 1 is a
charge to praise God in His sanctuary and in the expanse of His
power.…Verse 2 speaks of praising God for His mighty acts and
according to His vast greatness.…Verses 3 through 5 tell us to
praise God with the blast of the trumpet, the harp and lyre, the
tambourine and dancing, the stringed instrument and the pipe,
the loud cymbals, and the loud clanging cymbals. Today our spirit
is a much better "instrument" than any of the instruments mentioned in these verses. If we exercise our spirit, we will make good
"music."…Finally, verse 6 says that everything that has breath
should praise Jehovah. (*Life-study of the Psalms,* pp. 507-512)

Psalm 150 is not merely the conclusion of the Psalms; it is the
consummation of the entire Bible. The whole Bible ends in this
way. When we have read all the psalms, from Psalm 1 to Psalm
150, we have read from Genesis to Revelation in abbreviated
form, passing from the law, to Christ, to the house, and eventually
to the city with the earth. Then we have the Hallelujahs.

Revelation 19:1 says, "After these things I heard as it were a
loud voice of a great multitude in heaven, saying, Hallelujah!" This
is the conclusion of the Bible, just exactly like that of the Psalms.
(*Christ and the Church Revealed and Typified in the Psalms,* p. 222)

*Further Reading: Christ and the Church Revealed and Typified
in the Psalms,* ch. 22; *Life-study of the Psalms,* msgs. 44-45

**_Enlightenment and inspiration:_** _____
_____
_____
_____

## *Morning Nourishment*

Heb. **For it was fitting for Him, for whom are all things**
2:10 **and through whom are all things, in leading many**
**sons into glory, to make the Author of their salva-**
**tion perfect through sufferings.**
12 **Saying, "I will declare Your name to My brothers;**
**in the midst of the church I will sing hymns of**
**praise to You."**

All five books of the Psalms show us that the earth is the ultimate intention of God's desire. He must conquer the earth,
recover the earth, and bring it back under His rightful rule.

He must have the building up of the house and the city so that
He may recover the entire earth. This is our burden....There is
not one book, even in the New Testament, which reveals these
things so clearly as the Psalms.

The more we pray-read the Psalms, the more we see how
good it is that God has turned us from the law to Christ, that He
has brought us from Christ to the house, that we may be
enlarged from the house to the city, and that from the city He is
recovering the whole earth. Then God's purpose will be fulfilled.
Then we will all say, "O Jehovah our Lord, / How excellent is
Your name / In all the earth!" [Psa. 8:9]. Hallelujah! (*Christ and
the Church Revealed and Typified in the Psalms*, pp. 234-235)

## *Today's Reading*

The assembly [in Psalm 22:22] signifies the church, indicating
that the Lord's brothers constitute the church (Heb. 2:11-12).
Thus, His resurrection is the church-producing resurrection.
(Psa. 22:22, footnote 2)

*You* and *Your* in Psalm 22:22 refer to the Father. In resurrection
Christ declared the Father's name to His brothers and praised the
Father in the church (Heb. 2:12 and footnote 3). (Psa. 22:22, footnote 3)

Following his praise to God in the assembly, David advised
God's people to praise Jehovah and all the earth to worship Him

(Psa. 22:23-26, 29-31). Christ took the lead in praising God in the church, and the church follows Him to praise God. Now Israel should follow Christ and the church. (Psa. 22:23, footnote 1)

[Hebrews 2:12] is the firstborn Son's praising of the Father within the Father's many sons in the church meetings. When we, the many sons of God, meet as the church and praise the Father, the firstborn Son praises the Father in our praising. It is not that He praises the Father apart from us and alone; rather, He praises within us and with us through our praising. In our singing He sings hymns of praise to the Father. If then we do not sing, how can He sing? The more we sing to the Father, the more we enjoy His presence, His moving, His anointing, and His life-imparting within us. Thus we will grow in Him and be brought into His glorification above all. (Heb. 2:12, footnote 3)

Throughout all the centuries the firstborn Son has been continually singing hymns of praise unto the Father in the church.... Since He is in us, He sings praises unto the Father in our singing. His singing is in our singing. When we sing, He sings because He is within our singing. When we sing hymns to the Father from our spirit, He sings with us in our spirit. This is wonderful. The church on earth today is one corporate Body with the firstborn Son of God. In the meetings of the church, the firstborn Son of God sings praise to the Father. Whenever we come to the meetings, we must open our mouths to praise the Father. If we do this immediately, we cooperate with the indwelling firstborn Son of God.... The more we sing, the more He sings in our singing. The best way to have Christ work together with us is by singing praises to the Father. According to our experiences, many of us can testify that this is so. In some of the church meetings we did much singing to the Father. That was the time when we enjoyed Christ so much. We even had the sensation that He was singing in our singing. (*Life-study of Hebrews,* p. 139)

*Further Reading: Christ and the Church Revealed and Typified in the Psalms,* chs. 23-24; *Life-study of Hebrews,* msg. 12

### *Enlightenment and inspiration:* _____
_____
_____
_____

## *Morning Nourishment*

**Heb.** **Through Him then let us offer up a sacrifice of**
**13:15** **praise continually to God, that is, the fruit of lips**
**confessing His name.**
**Psa.** **Jehovah will reign forever, your God, O Zion, for-**
**146:10** **ever and ever. Hallelujah!**

To worship the Father, to worship God, is simply to present the Son of God. Either we present Christ to the Father, or we present Christ to others in the Father's presence—both are the best worship we can render to God. Real praise to the Father is not merely that we come to Him and say, "O Father, how great You are. You are so righteous, so holy, so high, so kind, and so good!" If we merely praise the Father in this way, we are rather religious. The real praises to the Father come out of our experience of Christ in our daily life....If we come to the meeting and say, "Hallelujah, Jesus is my Lord...," it seems that this is not praise to the Father. But I tell you, this is a very pleasing praise to the Father, gladdening and rejoicing His heart. (*How to Meet*, p. 164)

## *Today's Reading*

Hebrews 13:15 says, "Through Him then let us offer up a sacrifice of praise continually to God, that is, the fruit of lips confessing His name." This verse presents a profound thought. When we bear the reproach of Jesus and suffer on His behalf, we often groan and do not offer any praise to God. Yet the writer of the book of Hebrews tells us that when we pass through reproach and suffering, we should continually offer up a sacrifice of praise to God.

Verse 15 is a continuation of verses 8 through 14. Since in the church life we enjoy the unchanging Christ as grace and follow Him outside religion, we should offer through Him spiritual sacrifices to God. First, in the church we should offer up through Him a sacrifice of praise to God continually. In the church He sings in us hymns of praise unto God the Father (2:12). In the church we too should praise God the Father through Him. Eventually, in the church He and we, we and He, praise the Father together in the mingled spirit. Christ as the life-giving Spirit, praises the Father in our spirit, and we, by our spirit, praise the Father in His Spirit. This is the best and highest sacrifice that we can offer to God through Him. This is greatly needed in the church meetings.

Through the Christ whom we have experienced and enjoyed, we need to offer the sacrifice of praise to God continually. The real praise in the meetings must be constituted of our experiences of Christ. The sweetest praises we can offer to the Father are those we offer to Christ and which concern Christ. There is nothing more pleasant to the Father's heart than this. Real worship to the Father is the offering of His Son. In the preaching of the gospel, we tell the sinners that Christ is the Son of God, who redeemed us and who can save us and bring us to the Father. If we minister these things regarding Christ to the unbelievers, this is real worship to the Father. To worship God the Father is simply to present the Son of God. The real praise to the Father comes out of our experience of Christ in our daily life. This is a very pleasing praise to the Father, gladdening and rejoicing His heart. The Father desires that we glorify Him with the Son. If we glorify the Son, we glorify the Father. When we glorify the Son, the Father is glorified in His Son's being glorified by us (John 17:1). The praises out of our experience and enjoyment of Christ—the spiritual praises about Christ—are the best praise to the Father. (*The Conclusion of the New Testament,* pp. 3843-3844)

After passing through the first one hundred forty-five psalms, we are now on the peak. All we have to do now is to shout Hallelujah! The last five psalms—146, 147, 148, 149, and 150—begin and end in every case with Hallelujah. In these five psalms there are ten instances of Hallelujahs. Hallelujah, Hallelujah, Hallelujah! In these five psalms nothing new is presented. There is only praise, consummate praise. (*Christ and the Church Revealed and Typified in the Psalms,* p. 219)

*Further Reading: How to Meet,* chs. 16-18

### *Enlightenment and inspiration:* _____

_____
_____
_____

## *Hymns,* #1222

1    Sing aloud your praises to the Lord of all,
    Now He is dwelling in Jerusalem.
    Tell among us all His doings great and small,
    His throne, the heavens, yet He walks with men.
      Oh, the salvation out of Zion comes;
      He brought us back from our captivity.
      Now we rejoice and are exceeding glad;
      Now we rejoice and are exceeding glad!

2    In the Holy City with His own He dwells;
    O Lord, our Lord, how excellent Thy name!
    He's enthroned upon the praises of His saints;
    All His delight in Zion does remain.
      The local churches are His move today—
      He is our portion, we are satisfied.
      Oh, what a goodly heritage have we;
      Oh, what a goodly heritage have we!

3    Who shall in His holy tabernacle dwell,
    Who shall ascend to His most holy hill?
    Those who seek for Him and purify their heart;
    This generation now that seeks His face.
      Oh, seek His face, ye children of the earth,
      Open your heart, and let the King come in.
      He will come in, and He shall live and reign;
      He will come in, and He shall live and reign!

4    Look! God's tabernacle now is with the saints;
    Emmanuel—God with us, we proclaim.
    Everything is done, so let His children come;
    Christ and the church—where God and man are one!
      Lift up your heads, ye cities of the earth;
      Open your gates, and let the King come in.
      Shout to His praise—He's coming in to reign!
      Shout to His praise—He's coming in to reign!

*Composition for prophecy with main point and sub-points:* _____

# Reading Schedule for the Recovery Version of the Old Testament with Footnotes

| Wk. | Lord's Day | Monday | Tuesday | Wednesday | Thursday | Friday | Saturday |
|---|---|---|---|---|---|---|---|
| 1 | Gen 1:1-5 | 1:6-23 | 1:24-31 | 2:1-9 | 2:10-25 | 3:1-13 | 3:14-24 |
| 2 | 4:1-26 | 5:1-32 | 6:1-22 | 7:1—8:3 | 8:4-22 | 9:1-29 | 10:1-32 |
| 3 | 11:1-32 | 12:1-20 | 13:1-18 | 14:1-24 | 15:1-21 | 16:1-16 | 17:1-27 |
| 4 | 18:1-33 | 19:1-38 | 20:1-18 | 21:1-34 | 22:1-24 | 23:1—24:27 | 24:28-67 |
| 5 | 25:1-34 | 26:1-35 | 27:1-46 | 28:1-22 | 29:1-35 | 30:1-43 | 31:1-55 |
| 6 | 32:1-32 | 33:1—34:31 | 35:1-29 | 36:1-43 | 37:1-36 | 38:1—39:23 | 40:1—41:13 |
| 7 | 41:14-57 | 42:1-38 | 43:1-34 | 44:1-34 | 45:1-28 | 46:1-34 | 47:1-31 |
| 8 | 48:1-22 | 49:1-15 | 49:16-33 | 50:1-26 | Exo 1:1-22 | 2:1-25 | 3:1-22 |
| 9 | 4:1-31 | 5:1-23 | 6:1-30 | 7:1-25 | 8:1-32 | 9:1-35 | 10:1-29 |
| 10 | 11:1-10 | 12:1-14 | 12:15-36 | 12:37-51 | 13:1-22 | 14:1-31 | 15:1-27 |
| 11 | 16:1-36 | 17:1-16 | 18:1-27 | 19:1-25 | 20:1-26 | 21:1-36 | 22:1-31 |
| 12 | 23:1-33 | 24:1-18 | 25:1-22 | 25:23-40 | 26:1-14 | 26:15-37 | 27:1-21 |
| 13 | 28:1-21 | 28:22-43 | 29:1-21 | 29:22-46 | 30:1-10 | 30:11-38 | 31:1-17 |
| 14 | 31:18—32:35 | 33:1-23 | 34:1-35 | 35:1-35 | 36:1-38 | 37:1-29 | 38:1-31 |
| 15 | 39:1-43 | 40:1-38 | Lev 1:1-17 | 2:1-16 | 3:1-17 | 4:1-35 | 5:1-19 |
| 16 | 6:1-30 | 7:1-38 | 8:1-36 | 9:1-24 | 10:1-20 | 11:1-47 | 12:1-8 |
| 17 | 13:1-28 | 13:29-59 | 14:1-18 | 14:19-32 | 14:33-57 | 15:1-33 | 16:1-17 |
| 18 | 16:18-34 | 17:1-16 | 18:1-30 | 19:1-37 | 20:1-27 | 21:1-24 | 22:1-33 |
| 19 | 23:1-22 | 23:23-44 | 24:1-23 | 25:1-23 | 25:24-55 | 26:1-24 | 26:25-46 |
| 20 | 27:1-34 | Num 1:1-54 | 2:1-34 | 3:1-51 | 4:1-49 | 5:1-31 | 6:1-27 |
| 21 | 7:1-41 | 7:42-88 | 7:89—8:26 | 9:1-23 | 10:1-36 | 11:1-35 | 12:1—13:33 |
| 22 | 14:1-45 | 15:1-41 | 16:1-50 | 17:1—18:7 | 18:8-32 | 19:1-22 | 20:1-29 |
| 23 | 21:1-35 | 22:1-41 | 23:1-30 | 24:1-25 | 25:1-18 | 26:1-65 | 27:1-23 |
| 24 | 28:1-31 | 29:1-40 | 30:1—31:24 | 31:25-54 | 32:1-42 | 33:1-56 | 34:1-29 |
| 25 | 35:1-34 | 36:1-13 | Deut 1:1-46 | 2:1-37 | 3:1-29 | 4:1-49 | 5:1-33 |
| 26 | 6:1—7:26 | 8:1-20 | 9:1-29 | 10:1-22 | 11:1-32 | 12:1-32 | 13:1—14:21 |

## Reading Schedule for the Recovery Version of the Old Testament with Footnotes

| Wk. | Lord's Day | Monday | Tuesday | Wednesday | Thursday | Friday | Saturday |
|---|---|---|---|---|---|---|---|
| 27 | ☐ 14:22—15:23 | ☐ 16:1-22 | ☐ 17:1—18:8 | ☐ 18:9—19:21 | ☐ 20:1—21:17 | ☐ 21:18—22:30 | ☐ 23:1-25 |
| 28 | ☐ 24:1-22 | ☐ 25:1-19 | ☐ 26:1-19 | ☐ 27:1-26 | ☐ 28:1-68 | ☐ 29:1-29 | ☐ 30:1—31:29 |
| 29 | ☐ 31:30—32:52 | ☐ 33:1-29 | ☐ 34:1-12 | ☐ Josh 1:1-18 | ☐ 2:1-24 | ☐ 3:1-17 | ☐ 4:1-24 |
| 30 | ☐ 5:1-15 | ☐ 6:1-27 | ☐ 7:1-26 | ☐ 8:1-35 | ☐ 9:1-27 | ☐ 10:1-43 | ☐ 11:1—12:24 |
| 31 | ☐ 13:1-33 | ☐ 14:1—15:63 | ☐ 16:1—18:28 | ☐ 19:1-51 | ☐ 20:1—21:45 | ☐ 22:1-34 | ☐ 23:1—24:33 |
| 32 | ☐ Judg 1:1-36 | ☐ 2:1-23 | ☐ 3:1-31 | ☐ 4:1-24 | ☐ 5:1-31 | ☐ 6:1-40 | ☐ 7:1-25 |
| 33 | ☐ 8:1-35 | ☐ 9:1-57 | ☐ 10:1—11:40 | ☐ 12:1—13:25 | ☐ 14:1—15:20 | ☐ 16:1-31 | ☐ 17:1—18:31 |
| 34 | ☐ 19:1-30 | ☐ 20:1-48 | ☐ 21:1-25 | ☐ Ruth 1:1-22 | ☐ 2:1-23 | ☐ 3:1-18 | ☐ 4:1-22 |
| 35 | ☐ 1 Sam 1:1-28 | ☐ 2:1-36 | ☐ 3:1—4:22 | ☐ 5:1—6:21 | ☐ 7:1—8:22 | ☐ 9:1-27 | ☐ 10:1—11:15 |
| 36 | ☐ 12:1—13:23 | ☐ 14:1-52 | ☐ 15:1-35 | ☐ 16:1-23 | ☐ 17:1-58 | ☐ 18:1-30 | ☐ 19:1-24 |
| 37 | ☐ 20:1-42 | ☐ 21:1—22:23 | ☐ 23:1—24:22 | ☐ 25:1-44 | ☐ 26:1-25 | ☐ 27:1—28:25 | ☐ 29:1—30:31 |
| 38 | ☐ 31:1-13 | ☐ 2 Sam 1:1-27 | ☐ 2:1-32 | ☐ 3:1-39 | ☐ 4:1—5:25 | ☐ 6:1-23 | ☐ 7:1-29 |
| 39 | ☐ 8:1—9:13 | ☐ 10:1—11:27 | ☐ 12:1-31 | ☐ 13:1-39 | ☐ 14:1-33 | ☐ 15:1—16:23 | ☐ 17:1—18:33 |
| 40 | ☐ 19:1-43 | ☐ 20:1—21:22 | ☐ 22:1-51 | ☐ 23:1-39 | ☐ 24:1-25 | ☐ 1 Kings 1:1-19 | ☐ 1:20-53 |
| 41 | ☐ 2:1-46 | ☐ 3:1-28 | ☐ 4:1-34 | ☐ 5:1—6:38 | ☐ 7:1-22 | ☐ 7:23-51 | ☐ 8:1-36 |
| 42 | ☐ 8:37-66 | ☐ 9:1-28 | ☐ 10:1-29 | ☐ 11:1-43 | ☐ 12:1-33 | ☐ 13:1-34 | ☐ 14:1-31 |
| 43 | ☐ 15:1-34 | ☐ 16:1—17:24 | ☐ 18:1-46 | ☐ 19:1-21 | ☐ 20:1-43 | ☐ 21:1—22:53 | ☐ 2 Kings 1:1-18 |
| 44 | ☐ 2:1—3:27 | ☐ 4:1-44 | ☐ 5:1—6:33 | ☐ 7:1-20 | ☐ 8:1-29 | ☐ 9:1-37 | ☐ 10:1-36 |
| 45 | ☐ 11:1—12:21 | ☐ 13:1—14:29 | ☐ 15:1-38 | ☐ 16:1-20 | ☐ 17:1-41 | ☐ 18:1-37 | ☐ 19:1-37 |
| 46 | ☐ 20:1—21:26 | ☐ 22:1-20 | ☐ 23:1-37 | ☐ 24:1—25:30 | ☐ 1 Chron 1:1-54 | ☐ 2:1—3:24 | ☐ 4:1—5:26 |
| 47 | ☐ 6:1-81 | ☐ 7:1-40 | ☐ 8:1-40 | ☐ 9:1-44 | ☐ 10:1—11:47 | ☐ 12:1-40 | ☐ 13:1—14:17 |
| 48 | ☐ 15:1—16:43 | ☐ 17:1-27 | ☐ 18:1—19:19 | ☐ 20:1—21:30 | ☐ 22:1—23:32 | ☐ 24:1—25:31 | ☐ 26:1-32 |
| 49 | ☐ 27:1-34 | ☐ 28:1—29:30 | ☐ 2 Chron 1:1-17 | ☐ 2:1—3:17 | ☐ 4:1—5:14 | ☐ 6:1-42 | ☐ 7:1—8:18 |
| 50 | ☐ 9:1—10:19 | ☐ 11:1—12:16 | ☐ 13:1—15:19 | ☐ 16:1—17:19 | ☐ 18:1—19:11 | ☐ 20:1-37 | ☐ 21:1—22:12 |
| 51 | ☐ 23:1—24:27 | ☐ 25:1—26:23 | ☐ 27:1—28:27 | ☐ 29:1-36 | ☐ 30:1—31:21 | ☐ 32:1-33 | ☐ 33:1—34:33 |
| 52 | ☐ 35:1—36:23 | ☐ Ezra 1:1-11 | ☐ 2:1-70 | ☐ 3:1—4:24 | ☐ 5:1—6:22 | ☐ 7:1-28 | ☐ 8:1-36 |

# Reading Schedule for the Recovery Version of the Old Testament with Footnotes

| Wk. | Lord's Day | Monday | Tuesday | Wednesday | Thursday | Friday | Saturday |
|---|---|---|---|---|---|---|---|
| 53 | ☐ 9:1—10:44 | ☐ Neh 1:1-11 | ☐ 2:1—3:32 | ☐ 4:1—5:19 | ☐ 6:1-19 | ☐ 7:1-73 | ☐ 8:1-18 |
| 54 | ☐ 9:1-20 | ☐ 9:21-38 | ☐ 10:1—11:36 | ☐ 12:1-47 | ☐ 13:1-31 | ☐ Esth 1:1-22 | ☐ 2:1—3:15 |
| 55 | ☐ 4:1—5:14 | ☐ 6:1—7:10 | ☐ 8:1-17 | ☐ 9:1—10:3 | ☐ Job 1:1-22 | ☐ 2:1—3:26 | ☐ 4:1—5:27 |
| 56 | ☐ 6:1—7:21 | ☐ 8:1—9:35 | ☐ 10:1—11:20 | ☐ 12:1—13:28 | ☐ 14:1—15:35 | ☐ 16:1—17:16 | ☐ 18:1—19:29 |
| 57 | ☐ 20:1—21:34 | ☐ 22:1—23:17 | ☐ 24:1—25:6 | ☐ 26:1—27:23 | ☐ 28:1—29:25 | ☐ 30:1—31:40 | ☐ 32:1—33:33 |
| 58 | ☐ 34:1—35:16 | ☐ 36:1-33 | ☐ 37:1-24 | ☐ 38:1-41 | ☐ 39:1-30 | ☐ 40:1-24 | ☐ 41:1-34 |
| 59 | ☐ 42:1-17 | ☐ Psa 1:1-6 | ☐ 2:1—3:8 | ☐ 4:1—6:10 | ☐ 7:1—8:9 | ☐ 9:1—10:18 | ☐ 11:1—15:5 |
| 60 | ☐ 16:1—17:15 | ☐ 18:1-50 | ☐ 19:1—21:13 | ☐ 22:1-31 | ☐ 23:1—24:10 | ☐ 25:1—27:14 | ☐ 28:1—30:12 |
| 61 | ☐ 31:1—32:11 | ☐ 33:1—34:22 | ☐ 35:1—36:12 | ☐ 37:1-40 | ☐ 38:1—39:13 | ☐ 40:1—41:13 | ☐ 42:1—43:5 |
| 62 | ☐ 44:1-26 | ☐ 45:1-17 | ☐ 46:1—48:14 | ☐ 49:1—50:23 | ☐ 51:1—52:9 | ☐ 53:1—55:23 | ☐ 56:1—58:11 |
| 63 | ☐ 59:1—61:8 | ☐ 62:1—64:10 | ☐ 65:1—67:7 | ☐ 68:1-35 | ☐ 69:1—70:5 | ☐ 71:1—72:20 | ☐ 73:1—74:23 |
| 64 | ☐ 75:1—77:20 | ☐ 78:1-72 | ☐ 79:1—81:16 | ☐ 82:1—84:12 | ☐ 85:1—87:7 | ☐ 88:1—89:52 | ☐ 90:1—91:16 |
| 65 | ☐ 92:1—94:23 | ☐ 95:1—97:12 | ☐ 98:1—101:8 | ☐ 102:1—103:22 | ☐ 104:1—105:45 | ☐ 106:1-48 | ☐ 107:1-43 |
| 66 | ☐ 108:1—109:31 | ☐ 110:1—112:10 | ☐ 113:1—115:18 | ☐ 116:1—118:29 | ☐ 119:1-32 | ☐ 119:33-72 | ☐ 119:73-120 |
| 67 | ☐ 119:121-176 | ☐ 120:1—124:8 | ☐ 125:1—128:6 | ☐ 129:1—132:18 | ☐ 133:1—135:21 | ☐ 136:1—138:8 | ☐ 139:1—140:13 |
| 68 | ☐ 141:1—144:15 | ☐ 145:1—147:20 | ☐ 148:1—150:6 | ☐ Prov 1:1-33 | ☐ 2:1—3:35 | ☐ 4:1—5:23 | ☐ 6:1-35 |
| 69 | ☐ 7:1—8:36 | ☐ 9:1—10:32 | ☐ 11:1—12:28 | ☐ 13:1—14:35 | ☐ 15:1-33 | ☐ 16:1-33 | ☐ 17:1-28 |
| 70 | ☐ 18:1-24 | ☐ 19:1—20:30 | ☐ 21:1—22:29 | ☐ 23:1-35 | ☐ 24:1—25:28 | ☐ 26:1—27:27 | ☐ 28:1—29:27 |
| 71 | ☐ 30:1-33 | ☐ 31:1-31 | ☐ Eccl 1:1-18 | ☐ 2:1—3:22 | ☐ 4:1—5:20 | ☐ 6:1—7:29 | ☐ 8:1—9:18 |
| 72 | ☐ 10:1—11:10 | ☐ 12:1-14 | ☐ S.S 1:1-8 | ☐ 1:9-17 | ☐ 2:1-17 | ☐ 3:1-11 | ☐ 4:1-8 |
| 73 | ☐ 4:9-16 | ☐ 5:1-16 | ☐ 6:1-13 | ☐ 7:1-13 | ☐ 8:1-14 | ☐ Isa 1:1-11 | ☐ 1:12-31 |
| 74 | ☐ 2:1-22 | ☐ 3:1-26 | ☐ 4:1-6 | ☐ 5:1-30 | ☐ 6:1-13 | ☐ 7:1-25 | ☐ 8:1-22 |
| 75 | ☐ 9:1-21 | ☐ 10:1-34 | ☐ 11:1—12:6 | ☐ 13:1-22 | ☐ 14:1-14 | ☐ 14:15-32 | ☐ 15:1—16:14 |
| 76 | ☐ 17:1—18:7 | ☐ 19:1-25 | ☐ 20:1—21:17 | ☐ 22:1-25 | ☐ 23:1-18 | ☐ 24:1-23 | ☐ 25:1-12 |
| 77 | ☐ 26:1-21 | ☐ 27:1-13 | ☐ 28:1-29 | ☐ 29:1-24 | ☐ 30:1-33 | ☐ 31:1—32:20 | ☐ 33:1-24 |
| 78 | ☐ 34:1-17 | ☐ 35:1-10 | ☐ 36:1-22 | ☐ 37:1-38 | ☐ 38:1—39:8 | ☐ 40:1-31 | ☐ 41:1-29 |

## Reading Schedule for the Recovery Version of the Old Testament with Footnotes

| Wk. | Lord's Day | Monday | Tuesday | Wednesday | Thursday | Friday | Saturday |
|---|---|---|---|---|---|---|---|
| 79 | 42:1-25 | 43:1-28 | 44:1-28 | 45:1-25 | 46:1-13 | 47:1-15 | 48:1-22 |
| 80 | 49:1-13 | 49:14-26 | 50:1—51:23 | 52:1-15 | 53:1-12 | 54:1-17 | 55:1-13 |
| 81 | 56:1-12 | 57:1-21 | 58:1-14 | 59:1-21 | 60:1-22 | 61:1-11 | 62:1-12 |
| 82 | 63:1-19 | 64:1-12 | 65:1-25 | 66:1-24 | Jer 1:1-19 | 2:1-19 | 2:20-37 |
| 83 | 3:1-25 | 4:1-31 | 5:1-31 | 6:1-30 | 7:1-34 | 8:1-22 | 9:1-26 |
| 84 | 10:1-25 | 11:1—12:17 | 13:1-27 | 14:1-22 | 15:1-21 | 16:1—17:27 | 18:1-23 |
| 85 | 19:1—20:18 | 21:1—22:30 | 23:1-40 | 24:1—25:38 | 26:1—27:22 | 28:1—29:32 | 30:1-24 |
| 86 | 31:1-23 | 31:24-40 | 32:1-44 | 33:1-26 | 34:1-22 | 35:1-19 | 36:1-32 |
| 87 | 37:1-21 | 38:1-28 | 39:1—40:16 | 41:1—42:22 | 43:1—44:30 | 45:1—46:28 | 47:1—48:16 |
| 88 | 48:17-47 | 49:1-22 | 49:23-39 | 50:1-27 | 50:28-46 | 51:1-27 | 51:28-64 |
| 89 | 52:1-34 | Lam 1:1-22 | 2:1-22 | 3:1-39 | 3:40-66 | 4:1-22 | 5:1-22 |
| 90 | Ezek 1:1-14 | 1:15-28 | 2:1—3:27 | 4:1—5:17 | 6:1—7:27 | 8:1—9:11 | 10:1—11:25 |
| 91 | 12:1—13:23 | 14:1—15:8 | 16:1-63 | 17:1—18:32 | 19:1-14 | 20:1-49 | 21:1-32 |
| 92 | 22:1-31 | 23:1-49 | 24:1-27 | 25:1—26:21 | 27:1-36 | 28:1-26 | 29:1—30:26 |
| 93 | 31:1—32:32 | 33:1-33 | 34:1-31 | 35:1—36:21 | 36:22-38 | 37:1-28 | 38:1—39:29 |
| 94 | 40:1-27 | 40:28-49 | 41:1-26 | 42:1—43:27 | 44:1-31 | 45:1-25 | 46:1-24 |
| 95 | 47:1-23 | 48:1-35 | Dan 1:1-21 | 2:1-30 | 2:31-49 | 3:1-30 | 4:1-37 |
| 96 | 5:1-31 | 6:1-28 | 7:1-12 | 7:13-28 | 8:1-27 | 9:1-27 | 10:1-21 |
| 97 | 11:1-22 | 11:23-45 | 12:1-13 | Hosea 1:1-11 | 2:1-23 | 3:1—4:19 | 5:1-15 |
| 98 | 6:1-11 | 7:1-16 | 8:1-14 | 9:1-17 | 10:1-15 | 11:1-12 | 12:1-14 |
| 99 | 13:1—14:9 | Joel 1:1-20 | 2:1-16 | 2:17-32 | 3:1-21 | Amos 1:1-15 | 2:1-16 |
| 100 | 3:1-15 | 4:1—5:27 | 6:1—7:17 | 8:1—9:15 | Obad 1-21 | Jonah 1:1-17 | 2:1—4:11 |
| 101 | Micah 1:1-16 | 2:1—3:12 | 4:1—5:15 | 6:1—7:20 | Nahum 1:1-15 | 2:1—3:19 | Hab 1:1-17 |
| 102 | 2:1-20 | 3:1-19 | Zeph 1:1-18 | 2:1-15 | 3:1-20 | Hag 1:1-15 | 2:1-23 |
| 103 | Zech 1:1-21 | 2:1-13 | 3:1-10 | 4:1-14 | 5:1—6:15 | 7:1—8:23 | 9:1-17 |
| 104 | 10:1—11:17 | 12:1—13:9 | 14:1-21 | Mal 1:1-14 | 2:1-17 | 3:1-18 | 4:1-6 |

# Reading Schedule for the Recovery Version of the New Testament with Footnotes

| Wk. | Lord's Day | Monday | Tuesday | Wednesday | Thursday | Friday | Saturday |
|---|---|---|---|---|---|---|---|
| 1 | Matt 1:1-2 | 1:3-7 | 1:8-17 | 1:18-25 | 2:1-23 | 3:1-6 | 3:7-17 |
| 2 | 4:1-11 | 4:12-25 | 5:1-4 | 5:5-12 | 5:13-20 | 5:21-26 | 5:27-48 |
| 3 | 6:1-8 | 6:9-18 | 6:19-34 | 7:1-12 | 7:13-29 | 8:1-13 | 8:14-22 |
| 4 | 8:23-34 | 9:1-13 | 9:14-17 | 9:18-34 | 9:35—10:5 | 10:6-25 | 10:26-42 |
| 5 | 11:1-15 | 11:16-30 | 12:1-14 | 12:15-32 | 12:33-42 | 12:43—13:2 | 13:3-12 |
| 6 | 13:13-30 | 13:31-43 | 13:44-58 | 14:1-13 | 14:14-21 | 14:22-36 | 15:1-20 |
| 7 | 15:21-31 | 15:32-39 | 16:1-12 | 16:13-20 | 16:21-28 | 17:1-13 | 17:14-27 |
| 8 | 18:1-14 | 18:15-22 | 18:23-35 | 19:1-15 | 19:16-30 | 20:1-16 | 20:17-34 |
| 9 | 21:1-11 | 21:12-22 | 21:23-32 | 21:33-46 | 22:1-22 | 22:23-33 | 22:34-46 |
| 10 | 23:1-12 | 23:13-39 | 24:1-14 | 24:15-31 | 24:32-51 | 25:1-13 | 25:14-30 |
| 11 | 25:31-46 | 26:1-16 | 26:17-35 | 26:36-46 | 26:47-64 | 26:65-75 | 27:1-26 |
| 12 | 27:27-44 | 27:45-56 | 27:57—28:15 | 28:16-20 | Mark 1:1 | 1:2-6 | 1:7-13 |
| 13 | 1:14-28 | 1:29-45 | 2:1-12 | 2:13-28 | 3:1-19 | 3:20-35 | 4:1-25 |
| 14 | 4:26-41 | 5:1-20 | 5:21-43 | 6:1-29 | 6:30-56 | 7:1-23 | 7:24-37 |
| 15 | 8:1-26 | 8:27—9:1 | 9:2-29 | 9:30-50 | 10:1-16 | 10:17-34 | 10:35-52 |
| 16 | 11:1-16 | 11:17-33 | 12:1-27 | 12:28-44 | 13:1-13 | 13:14-37 | 14:1-26 |
| 17 | 14:27-52 | 14:53-72 | 15:1-15 | 15:16-47 | 16:1-8 | 16:9-20 | Luke 1:1-4 |
| 18 | 1:5-25 | 1:26-46 | 1:47-56 | 1:57-80 | 2:1-8 | 2:9-20 | 2:21-39 |
| 19 | 2:40-52 | 3:1-20 | 3:21-38 | 4:1-13 | 4:14-30 | 4:31-44 | 5:1-26 |
| 20 | 5:27—6:16 | 6:17-38 | 6:39-49 | 7:1-17 | 7:18-23 | 7:24-35 | 7:36-50 |
| 21 | 8:1-15 | 8:16-25 | 8:26-39 | 8:40-56 | 9:1-17 | 9:18-26 | 9:27-36 |
| 22 | 9:37-50 | 9:51-62 | 10:1-11 | 10:12-24 | 10:25-37 | 10:38-42 | 11:1-13 |
| 23 | 11:14-26 | 11:27-36 | 11:37-54 | 12:1-12 | 12:13-21 | 12:22-34 | 12:35-48 |
| 24 | 12:49-59 | 13:1-9 | 13:10-17 | 13:18-30 | 13:31—14:6 | 14:7-14 | 14:15-24 |
| 25 | 14:25-35 | 15:1-10 | 15:11-21 | 15:22-32 | 16:1-13 | 16:14-22 | 16:23-31 |
| 26 | 17:1-19 | 17:20-37 | 18:1-14 | 18:15-30 | 18:31-43 | 19:1-10 | 19:11-27 |

## Reading Schedule for the Recovery Version of the New Testament with Footnotes

| Wk. | Lord's Day | Monday | Tuesday | Wednesday | Thursday | Friday | Saturday |
|---|---|---|---|---|---|---|---|
| 27 | Luke 19:28-48 | 20:1-19 | 20:20-38 | 20:39—21:4 | 21:5-27 | 21:28-38 | 22:1-20 |
| 28 | 22:21-38 | 22:39-54 | 22:55-71 | 23:1-43 | 23:44-56 | 24:1-12 | 24:13-35 |
| 29 | 24:36-53 | John 1:1-13 | 1:14-18 | 1:19-34 | 1:35-51 | 2:1-11 | 2:12-22 |
| 30 | 2:23—3:13 | 3:14-21 | 3:22-36 | 4:1-14 | 4:15-26 | 4:27-42 | 4:43-54 |
| 31 | 5:1-16 | 5:17-30 | 5:31-47 | 6:1-15 | 6:16-31 | 6:32-51 | 6:52-71 |
| 32 | 7:1-9 | 7:10-24 | 7:25-36 | 7:37-52 | 7:53—8:11 | 8:12-27 | 8:28-44 |
| 33 | 8:45-59 | 9:1-13 | 9:14-34 | 9:35—10:9 | 10:10-30 | 10:31—11:4 | 11:5-22 |
| 34 | 11:23-40 | 11:41-57 | 12:1-11 | 12:12-24 | 12:25-36 | 12:37-50 | 13:1-11 |
| 35 | 13:12-30 | 13:31-38 | 14:1-6 | 14:7-20 | 14:21-31 | 15:1-11 | 15:12-27 |
| 36 | 16:1-15 | 16:16-33 | 17:1-5 | 17:6-13 | 17:14-24 | 17:25—18:11 | 18:12-27 |
| 37 | 18:28-40 | 19:1-16 | 19:17-30 | 19:31-42 | 20:1-13 | 20:14-18 | 20:19-22 |
| 38 | 20:23-31 | 21:1-14 | 21:15-22 | 21:23-25 | Acts 1:1-8 | 1:9-14 | 1:15-26 |
| 39 | 2:1-13 | 2:14-21 | 2:22-36 | 2:37-41 | 2:42-47 | 3:1-18 | 3:19—4:22 |
| 40 | 4:23-37 | 5:1-16 | 5:17-32 | 5:33-42 | 6:1—7:1 | 7:2-29 | 7:30-60 |
| 41 | 8:1-13 | 8:14-25 | 8:26-40 | 9:1-19 | 9:20-43 | 10:1-16 | 10:17-33 |
| 42 | 10:34-48 | 11:1-18 | 11:19-30 | 12:1-25 | 13:1-12 | 13:13-43 | 13:44—14:5 |
| 43 | 14:6-28 | 15:1-12 | 15:13-34 | 15:35—16:5 | 16:6-18 | 16:19-40 | 17:1-18 |
| 44 | 17:19-34 | 18:1-17 | 18:18-28 | 19:1-20 | 19:21-41 | 20:1-12 | 20:13-38 |
| 45 | 21:1-14 | 21:15-26 | 21:27-40 | 22:1-21 | 22:22-29 | 22:30—23:11 | 23:12-15 |
| 46 | 23:16-30 | 23:31—24:21 | 24:22—25:5 | 25:6-27 | 26:1-13 | 26:14-32 | 27:1-26 |
| 47 | 27:27—28:10 | 28:11-22 | 28:23-31 | Rom 1:1-2 | 1:3-7 | 1:8-17 | 1:18-25 |
| 48 | 1:26—2:10 | 2:11-29 | 3:1-20 | 3:21-31 | 4:1-12 | 4:13-25 | 5:1-11 |
| 49 | 5:12-17 | 5:18—6:5 | 6:6-11 | 6:12-23 | 7:1-12 | 7:13-25 | 8:1-2 |
| 50 | 8:3-6 | 8:7-13 | 8:14-25 | 8:26-39 | 9:1-18 | 9:19—10:3 | 10:4-15 |
| 51 | 10:16—11:10 | 11:11-22 | 11:23-36 | 12:1-3 | 12:4-21 | 13:1-14 | 14:1-12 |
| 52 | 14:13-23 | 15:1-13 | 15:14-33 | 16:1-5 | 16:6-24 | 16:25-27 | 1 Cor 1:1-4 |

## Reading Schedule for the Recovery Version of the New Testament with Footnotes

| Wk. | Lord's Day | Monday | Tuesday | Wednesday | Thursday | Friday | Saturday |
|---|---|---|---|---|---|---|---|
| 53 | 1 Cor 1:5-9 ☐ | 1:10-17 ☐ | 1:18-31 ☐ | 2:1-5 ☐ | 2:6-10 ☐ | 2:11-16 ☐ | 3:1-9 ☐ |
| 54 | 3:10-13 ☐ | 3:14-23 ☐ | 4:1-9 ☐ | 4:10-21 ☐ | 5:1-13 ☐ | 6:1-11 ☐ | 6:12-20 ☐ |
| 55 | 7:1-16 ☐ | 7:17-24 ☐ | 7:25-40 ☐ | 8:1-13 ☐ | 9:1-15 ☐ | 9:16-27 ☐ | 10:1-4 ☐ |
| 56 | 10:5-13 ☐ | 10:14-33 ☐ | 11:1-6 ☐ | 11:7-16 ☐ | 11:17-26 ☐ | 11:27-34 ☐ | 12:1-11 ☐ |
| 57 | 12:12-22 ☐ | 12:23-31 ☐ | 13:1-13 ☐ | 14:1-12 ☐ | 14:13-25 ☐ | 14:26-33 ☐ | 14:34-40 ☐ |
| 58 | 15:1-19 ☐ | 15:20-28 ☐ | 15:29-34 ☐ | 15:35-49 ☐ | 15:50-58 ☐ | 16:1-9 ☐ | 16:10-24 ☐ |
| 59 | 2 Cor 1:1-4 ☐ | 1:5-14 ☐ | 1:15-22 ☐ | 1:23—2:11 ☐ | 2:12-17 ☐ | 3:1-6 ☐ | 3:7-11 ☐ |
| 60 | 3:12-18 ☐ | 4:1-6 ☐ | 4:7-12 ☐ | 4:13-18 ☐ | 5:1-8 ☐ | 5:9-15 ☐ | 5:16-21 ☐ |
| 61 | 6:1-13 ☐ | 6:14—7:4 ☐ | 7:5-16 ☐ | 8:1-15 ☐ | 8:16-24 ☐ | 9:1-15 ☐ | 10:1-6 ☐ |
| 62 | 10:7-18 ☐ | 11:1-15 ☐ | 11:16-33 ☐ | 12:1-10 ☐ | 12:11-21 ☐ | 13:1-10 ☐ | 13:11-14 ☐ |
| 63 | Gal 1:1-5 ☐ | 1:6-14 ☐ | 1:15-24 ☐ | 2:1-13 ☐ | 2:14-21 ☐ | 3:1-4 ☐ | 3:5-14 ☐ |
| 64 | 3:15-22 ☐ | 3:23-29 ☐ | 4:1-7 ☐ | 4:8-20 ☐ | 4:21-31 ☐ | 5:1-12 ☐ | 5:13-21 ☐ |
| 65 | 5:22-26 ☐ | 6:1-10 ☐ | 6:11-15 ☐ | 6:16-18 ☐ | Eph 1:1-3 ☐ | 1:4-6 ☐ | 1:7-10 ☐ |
| 66 | 1:11-14 ☐ | 1:15-18 ☐ | 1:19-23 ☐ | 2:1-5 ☐ | 2:6-10 ☐ | 2:11-14 ☐ | 2:15-18 ☐ |
| 67 | 2:19-22 ☐ | 3:1-7 ☐ | 3:8-13 ☐ | 3:14-18 ☐ | 3:19-21 ☐ | 4:1-4 ☐ | 4:5-10 ☐ |
| 68 | 4:11-16 ☐ | 4:17-24 ☐ | 4:25-32 ☐ | 5:1-10 ☐ | 5:11-21 ☐ | 5:22-26 ☐ | 5:27-33 ☐ |
| 69 | 6:1-9 ☐ | 6:10-14 ☐ | 6:15-18 ☐ | 6:19-24 ☐ | Phil 1:1-7 ☐ | 1:8-18 ☐ | 1:19-26 ☐ |
| 70 | 1:27—2:4 ☐ | 2:5-11 ☐ | 2:12-16 ☐ | 2:17-30 ☐ | 3:1-6 ☐ | 3:7-11 ☐ | 3:12-16 ☐ |
| 71 | 3:17-21 ☐ | 4:1-9 ☐ | 4:10-23 ☐ | Col 1:1-8 ☐ | 1:9-13 ☐ | 1:14-23 ☐ | 1:24-29 ☐ |
| 72 | 2:1-7 ☐ | 2:8-15 ☐ | 2:16-23 ☐ | 3:1-4 ☐ | 3:5-15 ☐ | 3:16-25 ☐ | 4:1-18 ☐ |
| 73 | 1 Thes 1:1-3 ☐ | 1:4-10 ☐ | 2:1-12 ☐ | 2:13—3:5 ☐ | 3:6-13 ☐ | 4:1-10 ☐ | 4:11—5:11 ☐ |
| 74 | 5:12-28 ☐ | 2 Thes 1:1-12 ☐ | 2:1-17 ☐ | 3:1-18 ☐ | 1 Tim 1:1-2 ☐ | 1:3-4 ☐ | 1:5-14 ☐ |
| 75 | 1:15-20 ☐ | 2:1-7 ☐ | 2:8-15 ☐ | 3:1-13 ☐ | 3:14—4:5 ☐ | 4:6-16 ☐ | 5:1-25 ☐ |
| 76 | 6:1-10 ☐ | 6:11-21 ☐ | 2 Tim 1:1-10 ☐ | 1:11-18 ☐ | 2:1-15 ☐ | 2:16-26 ☐ | 3:1-13 ☐ |
| 77 | 3:14—4:8 ☐ | 4:9-22 ☐ | Titus 1:1-4 ☐ | 1:5-16 ☐ | 2:1-15 ☐ | 3:1-8 ☐ | 3:9-15 ☐ |
| 78 | Philem 1:1-11 ☐ | 1:12-25 ☐ | Heb 1:1-2 ☐ | 1:3-5 ☐ | 1:6-14 ☐ | 2:1-9 ☐ | 2:10-18 ☐ |

Psa. Let them praise the name of Jehovah, for
148:13 His name alone is exalted; His glory is
above the earth and the heavens.

150:1 Hallelujah! Praise God in His sanctuary;
praise Him in the expanse that *manifests*
His power.

6 Let everything that has breath praise Jehovah. Hallelujah!

*Date*

---

**Week 24 — Day 1**    **Today's verses**

Psa. Seven times a day I praise You for Your
119:164 righteous ordinances.

34:1 I will bless Jehovah at all times; His praise
will continually be in my mouth.

*Date*

---

Heb. For it was fitting for Him, for whom are all
2:10 things and through whom are all things, in
leading many sons into glory, to make the
Author of their salvation perfect through
sufferings.

12 Saying, "I will declare Your name to My
brothers; in the midst of the church I will
sing hymns of praise to You."

*Date*

---

**Week 24 — Day 2**    **Today's verses**

Exo. In Your lovingkindness You have led the
15:13 people whom You have redeemed; You
have guided them in Your strength to
Your holy habitation.

17-18 You will bring them in and plant them in
the mountain of Your inheritance, the
place, O Jehovah, which You have made
for Your dwelling, the sanctuary, O Lord,
which Your hands have established. Jehovah shall reign forever and ever.

*Date*

---

Heb. Through Him then let us offer up a sacri-
13:15 fice of praise continually to God, that is,
the fruit of lips confessing His name.

Psa. Jehovah will reign forever, your God, O
146:10 Zion, forever and ever. Hallelujah!

*Date*

---

**Week 24 — Day 3**    **Today's verses**

Psa. But You are holy, You who sit *enthroned*
22:3 upon the praises of Israel.

102:21 That the name of Jehovah may be declared in Zion, and His praise, in Jerusalem.

*Date*

# Reading Schedule for the Recovery Version of the New Testament with Footnotes

| Wk. | Lord's Day | Monday | Tuesday | Wednesday | Thursday | Friday | Saturday |
|---|---|---|---|---|---|---|---|
| 79 | ☐ Heb 3:1-6 | ☐ 3:7-19 | ☐ 4:1-9 | ☐ 4:10-13 | ☐ 4:14-16 | ☐ 5:1-10 | ☐ 5:11—6:3 |
| 80 | ☐ 6:4-8 | ☐ 6:9-20 | ☐ 7:1-10 | ☐ 7:11-28 | ☐ 8:1-6 | ☐ 8:7-13 | ☐ 9:1-4 |
| 81 | ☐ 9:5-14 | ☐ 9:15-28 | ☐ 10:1-18 | ☐ 10:19-28 | ☐ 10:29-39 | ☐ 11:1-6 | ☐ 11:7-19 |
| 82 | ☐ 11:20-31 | ☐ 11:32-40 | ☐ 12:1-2 | ☐ 12:3-13 | ☐ 12:14-17 | ☐ 12:18-26 | ☐ 12:27-29 |
| 83 | ☐ 13:1-7 | ☐ 13:8-12 | ☐ 13:13-15 | ☐ 13:16-25 | ☐ James 1:1-8 | ☐ 1:9-18 | ☐ 1:19-27 |
| 84 | ☐ 2:1-13 | ☐ 2:14-26 | ☐ 3:1-18 | ☐ 4:1-10 | ☐ 4:11-17 | ☐ 5:1-12 | ☐ 5:13-20 |
| 85 | ☐ 1 Pet 1:1-2 | ☐ 1:3-4 | ☐ 1:5 | ☐ 1:6-9 | ☐ 1:10-12 | ☐ 1:13-17 | ☐ 1:18-25 |
| 86 | ☐ 2:1-3 | ☐ 2:4-8 | ☐ 2:9-17 | ☐ 2:18-25 | ☐ 3:1-13 | ☐ 3:14-22 | ☐ 4:1-6 |
| 87 | ☐ 4:7-16 | ☐ 4:17-19 | ☐ 5:1-4 | ☐ 5:5-9 | ☐ 5:10-14 | ☐ 2 Pet 1:1-2 | ☐ 1:3-4 |
| 88 | ☐ 1:5-8 | ☐ 1:9-11 | ☐ 1:12-18 | ☐ 1:19-21 | ☐ 2:1-3 | ☐ 2:4-11 | ☐ 2:12-22 |
| 89 | ☐ 3:1-6 | ☐ 3:7-9 | ☐ 3:10-12 | ☐ 3:13-15 | ☐ 3:16 | ☐ 3:17-18 | ☐ 1 John 1:1-2 |
| 90 | ☐ 1:3-4 | ☐ 1:5 | ☐ 1:6 | ☐ 1:7 | ☐ 1:8-10 | ☐ 2:1-2 | ☐ 2:3-11 |
| 91 | ☐ 2:12-14 | ☐ 2:15-19 | ☐ 2:20-23 | ☐ 2:24-27 | ☐ 2:28-29 | ☐ 3:1-5 | ☐ 3:6-10 |
| 92 | ☐ 3:11-18 | ☐ 3:19-24 | ☐ 4:1-6 | ☐ 4:7-11 | ☐ 4:12-15 | ☐ 4:16—5:3 | ☐ 5:4-13 |
| 93 | ☐ 5:14-17 | ☐ 5:18-21 | ☐ 2 John 1:1-3 | ☐ 1:4-9 | ☐ 1:10-13 | ☐ 3 John 1:1-6 | ☐ 1:7-14 |
| 94 | ☐ Jude 1:1-4 | ☐ 1:5-10 | ☐ 1:11-19 | ☐ 1:20-25 | ☐ Rev 1:1-3 | ☐ 1:4-6 | ☐ 1:7-11 |
| 95 | ☐ 1:12-13 | ☐ 1:14-16 | ☐ 1:17-20 | ☐ 2:1-6 | ☐ 2:7 | ☐ 2:8-9 | ☐ 2:10-11 |
| 96 | ☐ 2:12-14 | ☐ 2:15-17 | ☐ 2:18-23 | ☐ 2:24-29 | ☐ 3:1-3 | ☐ 3:4-6 | ☐ 3:7-9 |
| 97 | ☐ 3:10-13 | ☐ 3:14-18 | ☐ 3:19-22 | ☐ 4:1-5 | ☐ 4:6-7 | ☐ 4:8-11 | ☐ 5:1-6 |
| 98 | ☐ 5:7-14 | ☐ 6:1-8 | ☐ 6:9-17 | ☐ 7:1-8 | ☐ 7:9-17 | ☐ 8:1-6 | ☐ 8:7-12 |
| 99 | ☐ 8:13—9:11 | ☐ 9:12-21 | ☐ 10:1-4 | ☐ 10:5-11 | ☐ 11:1-4 | ☐ 11:5-14 | ☐ 11:15-19 |
| 100 | ☐ 12:1-4 | ☐ 12:5-9 | ☐ 12:10-18 | ☐ 13:1-10 | ☐ 13:11-18 | ☐ 14:1-5 | ☐ 14:6-12 |
| 101 | ☐ 14:13-20 | ☐ 15:1-8 | ☐ 16:1-12 | ☐ 16:13-21 | ☐ 17:1-6 | ☐ 17:7-18 | ☐ 18:1-8 |
| 102 | ☐ 18:9—19:4 | ☐ 19:5-10 | ☐ 19:11-16 | ☐ 19:17-21 | ☐ 20:1-6 | ☐ 20:7-10 | ☐ 20:11-15 |
| 103 | ☐ 21:1 | ☐ 21:2 | ☐ 21:3-8 | ☐ 21:9-13 | ☐ 21:14-18 | ☐ 21:19-21 | ☐ 21:22-27 |
| 104 | ☐ 22:1 | ☐ 22:2 | ☐ 22:3-11 | ☐ 22:12-15 | ☐ 22:16-17 | ☐ 22:18-21 | |

## Week 19 — Day 4 — Today's verses

1 Pet. 2:4-5  Coming to Him, a living stone, rejected by men but with God chosen *and* precious, you yourselves also, as living stones, are being built up as a spiritual house into a holy priesthood to offer up spiritual sacrifices acceptable to God through Jesus Christ.

Psa. 118:25  O Jehovah, do save, we pray! O Jehovah, do send prosperity, we pray!

*Date*

## Week 19 — Day 5 — Today's verses

Matt. 16:18  And I also say to you that you are Peter, and upon this rock I will build My church, and the gates of Hades shall not prevail against it.

21:42  Jesus said to them, Have you never read in the Scriptures, "The stone which the builders rejected, this has become the head of the corner. This was from the Lord, and it is marvelous in our eyes"?

*Date*

## Week 19 — Day 6 — Today's verses

Matt. 5:14  You are the light of the world. It is impossible for a city situated upon a mountain to be hidden.

Psa. 118:26  Blessed is He who comes in the name of Jehovah; we bless you from the house of Jehovah.

*Date*

## Week 19 — Day 1 — Today's verses

Isa. 28:16  ...Indeed I lay a stone in Zion as a foundation, a tested stone, a precious cornerstone as a foundation firmly established; he who believes will not hasten away.

Acts 4:11-12  This is the stone which was considered as nothing by you, the builders, which has become the head of the corner. And there is salvation in no other, for neither is there another name under heaven given among men in which we must be saved.

*Date*

## Week 19 — Day 2 — Today's verses

Psa. 118:22  The stone which the builders rejected has become the head of the corner.

Eph. 2:21  In whom all the building, being fitted together, is growing into a holy temple in the Lord.

*Date*

## Week 19 — Day 3 — Today's verses

1 Pet. 2:6-7  ..."Behold, I lay in Zion a cornerstone, chosen *and* precious; and he who believes on Him shall by no means be put to shame." To you therefore who believe is the preciousness; but to the unbelieving, "The stone which the builders rejected, this has become the head of the corner."

Psa. 118:24  This is the day that Jehovah has made; let us exult and rejoice in it.

*Date*

## Week 20 — Day 4  Today's verses

Rom. That the righteous requirement of the law
8:4  might be fulfilled in us, who do not walk
according to the flesh but according to
the spirit.

Exo. ...You shall not boil a kid in its mother's
23:19 milk.

*Date*

## Week 20 — Day 5  Today's verses

Psalm  Deal bountifully with Your servant that I
119:17-18 may live and keep Your word. Open my
eyes that I may behold wondrous things
out of Your law.

105  Your word is a lamp to my feet and a light to
my path.

127  Therefore I love Your commandments more
than gold, indeed, more than fine gold.

*Date*

## Week 20 — Day 6  Today's verses

Psa. And I will lift up my hand to Your com-
119:48 mandments, which I love; and I will muse
upon Your statutes.

147-148 I anticipated the dawn and cried out; I
hoped in Your words. My eyes anticipated
the night watches, that I might muse upon
Your word.

162  I rejoice at Your word, like one who finds
great spoil.

*Date*

## Week 20 — Day 1  Today's verses

Exo. And he was there with Jehovah forty days
34:28 and forty nights; he did not eat bread, and
he did not drink water. And He wrote
upon the tablets the words of the covenant, the Ten Commandments.

2 Tim. All Scripture is God-breathed and profit-
3:16-17 able for teaching, for conviction, for correction, for instruction in righteousness,
that the man of God may be complete,
fully equipped for every good work.

Rev. ...His name is called the Word of God.
19:13

*Date*

## Week 20 — Day 2  Today's verses

2 Cor. Who has also made us sufficient as minis-
3:6  ters of a new covenant, *ministers* not of
the letter but of the Spirit; for the letter
kills, but the Spirit gives life.

Psa. ...I love Your commandments more than
119:127 gold, indeed, more than fine gold.

130  The opening of Your words gives light,
imparting understanding to the simple.

*Date*

## Week 20 — Day 3  Today's verses

Psa. The law of Jehovah is perfect, restoring the
19:7-8 soul; the testimony of Jehovah is faithful,
making the simple wise; the precepts of Jehovah are right, making the heart joyous;
the commandment of Jehovah is clear, enlightening the eyes.

119:25 ...Enliven me according to Your word.

103  How sweet are Your words to my taste!
Sweeter than honey to my mouth!

*Date*

| Week 21 — Day 4 | Today's verses | Week 21 — Day 5 | Today's verses | Week 21 — Day 6 | Today's verses |
|---|---|---|---|---|---|
| Psa. 127:1-2 | Unless Jehovah builds the house, those who build it labor in vain. Unless Jehovah keeps the city, the guard watches in vain. It is vain for you to rise up early, to stay up late, to eat the bread of toil; all the same, He gives to His beloved while they sleep. | Psa. 128:5 | Jehovah bless you from Zion; and may you see the prosperity of Jerusalem all the days of your life. | Psa. 132:8-9 | Arise, O Jehovah, unto Your resting place, You and the Ark of Your strength. Let Your priests be clothed with righteousness, and let Your faithful ones give a ringing shout. |
| | | Psa. 131:1-2 | O Jehovah, my heart is not proud, nor are my eyes haughty; nor do I go about in things too great or too wondrous for me. Surely I have calmed and quieted my soul, like a weaned child with its mother; like a weaned child is my soul within me. | | |

_____
Date

_____
Date

_____
Date

| Week 21 — Day 1 | Today's verses | Week 21 — Day 2 | Today's verses | Week 21 — Day 3 | Today's verses |
|---|---|---|---|---|---|
| Psa. 2:6 | But I have installed My King upon Zion, My holy mountain. | Rev. 14:1 | And I saw, and behold, the Lamb standing on Mount Zion, and with Him a hundred and forty-four thousand, having His name and the name of His Father written on their foreheads. | Rev. 19:7 | Let us rejoice and exult, and let us give the glory to Him, for the marriage of the Lamb has come, and His wife has made herself ready. |
| 125:1-2 | Those who trust in Jehovah are like Mount Zion, which cannot be moved but abides forever. Jerusalem—mountains surround her; and Jehovah surrounds His people from now and to eternity. | 12:11 | And they overcame him because of the blood of the Lamb and because of the word of their testimony, and they loved not their soul-life even unto death. | 1 Tim. 2:8 | I desire therefore that men pray in every place, lifting up holy hands, without wrath and reasoning. |

_____
Date

_____
Date

_____
Date

| Week 22 — Day 4 | Today's verses | Week 22 — Day 5 | Today's verses | Week 22 — Day 6 | Today's verses |
|---|---|---|---|---|---|

Week 22 — Day 4    Today's verses

Psa. Behold, how good and how pleasant it is
133:1-3 for brothers to dwell in unity! It is like the fine oil upon the head that ran down upon the beard, upon Aaron's beard, that ran down upon the hem of his garments; like the dew of Hermon that came down upon the mountains of Zion. For there Jehovah commanded the blessing: life forever.

*Date*

Week 22 — Day 5    Today's verses

Acts And with great power the apostles gave
4:33 testimony of the resurrection of the Lord Jesus, and great grace was upon them all.

1 Tim. And the grace of our Lord superabounded
1:14 with faith and love in Christ Jesus.

Rom. …Those who receive the abundance of
5:17 grace and of the gift of righteousness will reign in life through the One, Jesus Christ.

*Date*

Week 22 — Day 6    Today's verses

Psa. Bless Jehovah now, all you servants of Je-
134:1-3 hovah who stand by night in the house of Jehovah. Lift up your hands in the sanctuary, and bless Jehovah. May Jehovah, who made heaven and earth, bless you from Zion.

*Date*

Week 22 — Day 1    Today's verses

Psa. For Jehovah has chosen Zion; He has de-
132:13-16 sired it for His habitation. This is My resting place forever; here will I dwell, for I have desired it. I will abundantly bless its provision; I will satisfy its poor with bread. And its priests I will clothe with salvation, and its faithful ones will shout with a ringing shout.

133:1 Behold, how good and how pleasant it is for brothers to dwell in unity!

*Date*

Week 22 — Day 2    Today's verses

Eph. Being diligent to keep the oneness of the
4:3-6 Spirit in the uniting bond of peace: one Body and one Spirit, even as also you were called in one hope of your calling; one Lord, one faith, one baptism; one God and Father of all, who is over all and through all and in all.

*Date*

Week 22 — Day 3    Today's verses

Exo. You also take the finest spices: of flowing
30:23-25 myrrh… and of fragrant cinnamon…and of fragrant calamus…and of cassia…and a hin of olive oil. And you shall make it a holy anointing oil, a fragrant ointment compounded…

Phil. For I know that for me this will turn out to
1:19 salvation through your petition and *the* bountiful supply of the Spirit of Jesus Christ.

*Date*

## Week 23 — Day 4 — Today's verses

Psa. Ask of Me, and I will give the nations as
2:8-9 Your inheritance and the limits of the earth as Your possession. You will break them with an iron rod...

8:1-2 O Jehovah our Lord, how excellent is Your name in all the earth, You who have set Your glory over the heavens! Out of the mouths of babes and sucklings You have established strength because of Your adversaries, to stop the enemy and the avenger.

*Date* _____

## Week 23 — Day 5 — Today's verses

Psa. The earth is Jehovah's, and its fullness, the
24:1 habitable land and those who dwell in it.

47:2 For Jehovah Most High is awesome: a great King over all the earth.

*Date* _____

## Week 23 — Day 6 — Today's verses

Psa. ...Jehovah...is coming to judge the earth;
96:13 He will judge the world with righteousness, and the peoples with His truth.

97:1 Jehovah reigns! Let the earth be glad; let the many islands rejoice.

145:11-13 They will speak of the glory of Your kingdom....to make known...the glorious splendor of Your kingdom. Your kingdom is an eternal kingdom...

*Date* _____

## Week 23 — Day 1 — Today's verses

Luke ...All the things written in the Law of Moses
24:44 and the Prophets and Psalms concerning Me must be fulfilled.

Gen. And God said, Let Us make man in Our im-
1:26 age, according to Our likeness; and let them have dominion...

Rev. ...The kingdom of the world has become
11:15 the *kingdom* of our Lord and of His Christ, and He will reign forever and ever.

19:10 ...The testimony of Jesus is the spirit of the prophecy.

*Date* _____

## Week 23 — Day 2 — Today's verses

Gen. ...Let Us make man in Our image, accord-
1:26-28 ing to Our likeness; and let them have dominion...over all the earth and over every creeping thing that creeps upon the earth. And God created man in His own image; in the image of God He created him; male and female He created them. And God blessed them; and God said to them, Be fruitful and multiply, and fill the earth and subdue it, and have dominion...over every living thing that moves upon the earth.

*Date* _____

## Week 23 — Day 3 — Today's verses

Matt. You then pray in this way: Our Father who is
6:9-10 in the heavens, Your name be sanctified; Your kingdom come; Your will be done, as in heaven, so also on earth.

13 ...For Yours is the kingdom and the power and the glory forever. Amen.

*Date* _____